Enterprise Data Workflows with Cascading

Paco Nathan

Beijing · Cambridge · Farnham · Köln · Sebastopol · Tokyo

Enterprise Data Workflows with Cascading

by Paco Nathan

Published by O'Reilly Media, Inc., 1005 Gravenstein Highway North, Sebastopol, CA 95472.

O'Reilly books may be purchased for educational, business, or sales promotional use. Online editions are also available for most titles (*http://my.safaribooksonline.com*). For more information, contact our corporate/institutional sales department: 800-998-9938 or *corporate@oreilly.com*.

Editors: Mike Loukides and Courtney Nash	**Indexer:** Paco Nathan
Production Editor: Kristen Borg	**Cover Designer:** Randy Comer
Copyeditor: Kim Cofer	**Interior Designer:** David Futato
Proofreader: Julie Van Keuren	**Illustrator:** Rebecca Demarest

July 2013:   First Edition

Revision History for the First Edition:

2013-07-10:   First release

See *http://oreilly.com/catalog/errata.csp?isbn=9781449358723* for release details.

ISBN: 978-1-449-35872-3

[LSI]

Table of Contents

Preface

Requirements

Throughout this book, we will explore Cascading and related open source projects in the context of brief programming examples. Familiarity with Java programming is required. We'll show additional code in Clojure, Scala, SQL, and R. The sample apps are all available in source code repositories on GitHub (*https://github.com/Cascading*). These sample apps are intended to run on a laptop (Linux, Unix, and Mac OS X, but not Windows) using Apache Hadoop in standalone mode. Each example is built so that it will run efficiently with a large data set on a large cluster, but setting new world records on Hadoop isn't our agenda. Our intent here is to introduce a new way of thinking about how Enterprise apps get designed. We will show how to get started with Cascading and discuss best practices for Enterprise data workflows.

Enterprise Data Workflows

Cascading provides an open source API for writing Enterprise-scale apps on top of Apache Hadoop and other Big Data frameworks. In production use now for five years (as of 2013Q1), Cascading apps run at hundreds of different companies and in several verticals, which include finance, retail, health care, and transportation. Case studies have been published about large deployments at Williams-Sonoma, Twitter, Etsy, Airbnb, Square, The Climate Corporation, Nokia, Factual, uSwitch, Trulia, Yieldbot, and the Harvard School of Public Health. Typical use cases for Cascading include large extract/transform/load (ETL) jobs (*http://bit.ly/17THIHk*), reporting, web crawlers, anti-fraud classifiers, social recommender systems, retail pricing, climate analysis, geolocation, genomics, plus a variety of other kinds of machine learning and optimization problems.

Keep in mind that Apache Hadoop rarely if ever gets used in isolation. Generally speaking, apps that run on Hadoop must consume data from a variety of sources, and in turn they produce data that must be used in other frameworks. For example, a hypothetical social recommender shown in Figure P-1 combines input data from customer profiles in a distributed database plus log files from a cluster of web servers, then moves its recommendations out to Memcached to be served through an API. Cascading encompasses the schema and dependencies for each of those components in a workflow—data sources for input, business logic in the application, the flows that define parallelism, rules for handling exceptions, data sinks for end uses, etc. The problem at hand is much more complex than simply a sequence of Hadoop job steps.

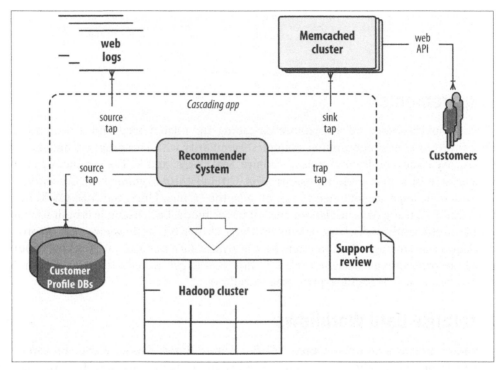

Figure P-1. Example social recommender

Moreover, while Cascading has been closely associated with Hadoop, it is not tightly coupled to it. Flow planners exist for other topologies beyond Hadoop, such as in-memory data grids for real-time workloads. That way a given app could compute some parts of a workflow in batch and some in real time, while representing a consistent "unit of work" for scheduling, accounting, monitoring, etc. The system integration of many different frameworks means that Cascading apps define comprehensive workflows.

Circa early 2013, many Enterprise organizations are building out their Hadoop practices. There are several reasons, but for large firms the compelling reasons are mostly economic. Let's consider a typical scenario for Enterprise data workflows prior to Hadoop, shown in Figure P-2.

An analyst typically would make a SQL query in a data warehouse such as Oracle or Teradata to pull a data set. That data set might be used directly for a pivot tables in Excel for ad hoc queries, or as a data cube going into a business intelligence (BI) server such as Microstrategy for reporting. In turn, a stakeholder such as a product owner would consume that analysis via dashboards, spreadsheets, or presentations. Alternatively, an analyst might use the data in an analytics platform such as SAS for predictive modeling, which gets handed off to a developer for building an application. Ops runs the apps, manages the data warehouse (among other things), and oversees ETL jobs that load data from other sources. Note that in this diagram there are multiple components—data warehouse, BI server, analytics platform, ETL—which have relatively expensive licensing and require relatively expensive hardware. Generally these apps "scale up" by purchasing larger and more expensive licenses and hardware.

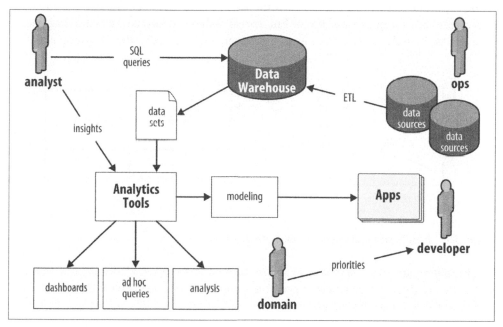

Figure P-2. Enterprise data workflows, pre-Hadoop

Circa late 1997 there was an inflection point, after which a handful of pioneering Internet companies such as Amazon and eBay began using "machine data"—that is to say, data gleaned from distributed logs that had mostly been ignored before—to build large-scale data apps based on clusters of "commodity" hardware. Prices for disk-based storage and commodity servers dropped considerably, while many uses for large clusters began to arise. Apache Hadoop derives from the MapReduce project at Google, which was part of this inflection point. More than a decade later, we see widespread adoption of Hadoop in Enterprise use cases. On one hand, generally these use cases "scale out" by running workloads in parallel on clusters of commodity hardware, leveraging mostly open source software. That mitigates the rising cost of licenses and proprietary hardware as data rates grow enormously. On the other hand, this practice imposes an interesting change in business process: notice how in Figure P-3 the developers with Hadoop expertise become a new kind of bottleneck for analysts and operations.

Enterprise adoption of Apache Hadoop, driven by huge savings and opportunities for new kinds of large-scale data apps, has increased the need for experienced Hadoop programmers disproportionately. There's been a big push to train current engineers and analysts and to recruit skilled talent. However, the skills required to write large Hadoop apps directly in Java are difficult to learn for most developers and far outside the norm of expectations for analysts. Consequently the approach of attempting to retrain current staff does not scale very well. Meanwhile, companies are finding that the process of hiring expert Hadoop programmers is somewhere in the range of difficult to impossible. That creates a dilemma for staffing, as Enterprise rushes to embrace Big Data and Apache Hadoop: SQL analysts are available and relatively less expensive than Hadoop experts.

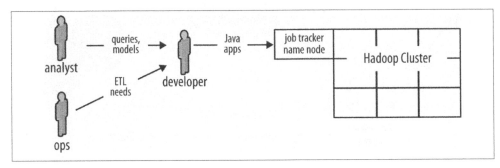

Figure P-3. Enterprise data workflows, with Hadoop

An alternative approach is to use an abstraction layer on top of Hadoop—one that fits well with existing Java practices. Several leading IT publications have described Cascading in those terms, for example:

> Management can really go out and build a team around folks that are already very experienced with Java. Switching over to this is really a very short exercise.
>
> — Thor Olavsrud
> *CIO magazine (2012)*

Cascading recently added support for ANSI SQL through a library called Lingual. Another library called Pattern supports the Predictive Model Markup Language (PMML) (*http://en.wikipedia.org/wiki/Predictive_Model_Markup_Language*), which is used by most major analytics and BI platforms to export data mining models. Through these extensions, Cascading provides greater access to Hadoop resources for the more traditional analysts as well as Java developers. Meanwhile, other projects atop Cascading —such as Scalding (based on Scala) and Cascalog (based on Clojure)—are extending highly sophisticated software engineering practices to Big Data. For example, Cascalog provides features for test-driven development (TDD) (*http://en.wikipedia.org/wiki/Test-driven_development*) of Enterprise data workflows.

Complexity, More So Than Bigness

It's important to note that a tension exists between complexity and innovation, which is ultimately driven by scale. Closely related to that dynamic, a spectrum emerges about technologies that manage data, ranging from "conservatism" to "liberalism."

Consider that technology start-ups rarely follow a straight path from initial concept to success. Instead they tend to pivot through different approaches and priorities before finding market traction. The book *Lean Startup* (*http://theleanstartup.com/*) by Eric Ries (Crown Business) articulates the process in detail. Flexibility is key to avoiding disaster; one of the biggest liabilities a start-up faces is that it cannot change rapidly enough to pivot toward potential success—or that it will run out of money before doing so. Many start-ups choose to use Ruby on Rails, Node.js, Python, or PHP because of the flexibility those scripting languages allow.

On one hand, technology start-ups tend to crave complexity; they want and need the problems associated with having many millions of customers. Providing services so mainstream and vital that regulatory concerns come into play is typically a nice problem to have. Most start-ups will never reach that stage of business or that level of complexity in their apps; however, many will try to innovate their way toward it. A start-up typically wants no impediments—that is where the "liberalism" aspects come in. In many ways, Facebook exemplifies this approach; the company emerged through intense customer experimentation, and it retains that aspect of a start-up even after enormous growth.

A Political Spectrum for Programming

Consider the arguments this article (*http://bit.ly/12GSJ5R*) presents about software "liberalism" versus "conservatism":

> Just as in real-world politics, software conservatism and liberalism are radically different world views. Make no mistake: they are at odds. They have opposing value systems, priorities, core beliefs and motivations. These value systems clash at design time, at implementation time, at diagnostic time, at recovery time. They get along like green eggs and ham.

> — Steve Yegge
> *Notes from the Mystery Machine Bus*
> *(2012)*

This spectrum is encountered in the use of Big Data frameworks, too. On the "liberalism" end of the spectrum, there are mostly start-ups—plus a few notable large firms, such as Facebook. On the "conservatism" end of the spectrum there is mostly Enterprise—plus a few notable start-ups, such as The Climate Corporation.

On the other hand, you probably don't want your bank to run customer experiments on your checking account, not anytime soon. Enterprise differs from start-ups because of the complexities of large, existing business units. Keeping a business running smoothly is a complex problem, especially in the context of aggressive competition and rapidly changing markets. Generally there are large liabilities for mishandling data: regulatory and compliance issues, bad publicity, loss of revenue streams, potential litigation, stock market reactions, etc. Enterprise firms typically want no surprises, and predictability is key to avoiding disaster. That is where the "conservatism" aspects come in.

Enterprise organizations must live with complexity 24/7, but they crave innovation. Your bank, your airline, your hospital, the power plant on the other side of town—those have risk profiles based on "conservatism." Computing environments in Enterprise IT typically use Java virtual machine (JVM) (*http://en.wikipedia.org/wiki/Java_virtual_machine*) languages such as Java, Scala, Clojure, etc. In some cases scripting languages are banned entirely. Recognize that this argument is not about political views; rather, it's about how to approach complexity. The risk profile for a business vertical tends to have a lot of influence on its best practices.

Trade-offs among programming languages and abstractions used in Big Data exist along these fault lines of flexibility versus predictability. In the "liberalism" camp, Apache Hive and Pig have become popular abstractions on top of Apache Hadoop. Early adopters of MapReduce programming tended to focus on ad hoc queries and proof-of-concept apps. They placed great emphasis on programming flexibility. Needing to explore a large unstructured data set through ad hoc queries was a much more common priority than, say, defining an Enterprise data workflow for a mission-critical app. In environments where scripting languages (Ruby, Python, PHP, Perl, etc.) run in production, scripting tools such as Hive and Pig have been popular Hadoop abstractions. They provide lots of flexibility and work well for performing ad hoc queries at scale.

Relatively speaking, circa 2013, it is not difficult to load a few terabytes of unstructured data into an Apache Hadoop cluster and then run SQL-like queries in Hive. Difficulties emerge when you must make frequent updates to the data, or schedule mission-critical apps, or run many apps simultaneously. Also, as workflows integrate Hive apps with other frameworks outside of Hadoop, those apps gain additional complexity: parts of the business logic are declared in SQL, while other parts are represented in another programming language and paradigm. Developing and debugging complex workflows becomes expensive for Enterprise organizations, because each issue may require hours or even days before its context can be reproduced within a test environment.

A fundamental issue is that the difficulty of operating at scale is not so much a matter of *bigness* in data; rather, it's a matter of managing *complexity* within the data. For companies that are just starting to embrace Big Data, the software development lifecycle (SDLC) (*http://en.wikipedia.org/wiki/Systems_development_life-cycle*) itself becomes the hard problem to solve. That difficulty is compounded by the fact that hiring and training programmers to write MapReduce code directly is already a bitter pill for most companies.

Table P-1 shows a pattern of migration, from the typical "legacy" toolsets used for large-scale batch workflows—such as J2EE and SQL—into the adoption of Apache Hadoop and related frameworks for Big Data.

Table P-1. Migration of batch toolsets

Workflow	Legacy	Manage complexity	Early adopter
Pipelines	J2EE	Cascading	Pig
Queries	SQL	Lingual (ANSI SQL)	Hive
Predictive models	SAS	Pattern (PMML)	Mahout

As more Enterprise organizations move to use Apache Hadoop for their apps, typical Hadoop workloads shift from early adopter needs toward mission-critical operations. Typical risk profiles are shifting toward "conservatism" in programming environments. Cascading provides a popular solution for defining and managing Enterprise data workflows. It provides predictability and accountability for the physical plan of a workflow and mitigates difficulties in handling exceptions, troubleshooting bugs, optimizing code, testing at scale, etc.

Also keep in mind the issue of how the needs for a start-up business evolve over time. For the firms working on the "liberalism" end of this spectrum, as they grow there is often a need to migrate into toolsets that are more toward the "conservatism" end. A large code base that has been originally written based on using Pig or Hive can be considerably difficult to migrate. Alternatively, writing that same functionality in a framework such as Cascalog would provide flexibility for the early phase of the start-up, while mitigating complexity as the business grows.

Origins of the Cascading API

In the mid-2000s, Chris Wensel was a system architect at an Enterprise firm known for its data products, working on a custom search engine for case law. He had been working with open source code from the Nutch project, which gave him early hands-on experience with popular spin-offs from Nutch: Lucene and Hadoop. On one hand, Wensel recognized that Hadoop had great potential for indexing large sets of documents, which was core business at his company. On the other hand, Wensel could foresee that coding in Hadoop's MapReduce API directly would be difficult for many programmers to learn and would not likely scale for widespread adoption.

Moreover, the requirements for Enterprise firms to adopt Hadoop—or for any programming abstraction atop Hadoop—would be on the "conservatism" end of the spectrum. For example, indexing case law involves large, complex ETL workflows, with substantial liability if incorrect data gets propagated through the workflow and downstream to users. Those apps must be solid, data provenance must be auditable, workflow responses to failure modes must be deterministic, etc. In this case, Ops would not allow solutions based on scripting languages.

Late in 2007, Wensel began to write Cascading as an open source application framework for Java developers to develop robust apps on Hadoop, quickly and easily. From the beginning, the project was intended to provide a set of abstractions in terms of database primitives and the analogy of "plumbing." Cascading addresses complexity while embodying the "conservatism" of Enterprise IT best practices. The abstraction is effective on several levels: capturing business logic, implementing complex algorithms, specifying system dependencies, projecting capacity needs, etc. In addition to the Java API, support for several other languages has been built atop Cascading, as shown in Figure P-4.

Formally speaking, Cascading represents a pattern language (*http://en.wikipedia.org/wiki/Pattern_language*) for the business process management of Enterprise data workflows. Pattern languages provide structured methods for solving large, complex design problems—where the syntax of the language promotes use of best practices. For example, the "plumbing" metaphor of pipes and operators in Cascading helps indicate which algorithms should be used at particular points, which architectural trade-offs are appropriate, where frameworks need to be integrated, etc.

One benefit of this approach is that many potential problems can get caught at compile time or at the flow planner stage. Cascading follows the principle of "Plan far ahead." Due to the functional constraints imposed by Cascading, flow planners generally detect errors long before an app begins to consume expensive resources on a large cluster. Or in another sense, long before an app begins to propagate the wrong results downstream.

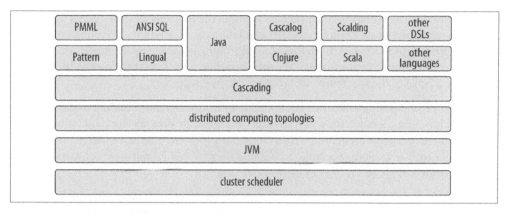

Figure P-4. Cascading technology stack

Also in late 2007, Yahoo! Research moved the Pig project to the Apache Incubator. Pig and Cascading are interesting to contrast, because newcomers to Hadoop technologies often compare the two. Pig represents a data manipulation language (DML) (*http://en.wikipedia.org/wiki/Data_manipulation_language*), which provides a query algebra atop Hadoop. It is not an API for a JVM language, nor does it specify a pattern language. Another important distinction is that Pig attempts to perform optimizations on a logical plan, whereas Cascading uses a physical plan only. The former is great for early adopter use cases, ad hoc queries, and less complex applications. The latter is great for Enterprise data workflows, where IT places a big premium on "no surprises."

In the five years since 2007, there have been two major releases of Cascading and hundreds of Enterprise deployments. Programming with the Cascading API can be done in a variety of JVM-based languages: Java, Scala, Clojure, Python (Jython), and Ruby (JRuby). Of these, Scala and Clojure have become the most popular for large deployments.

Several other open source projects, such as DSLs, taps, libraries, etc., have been written based on Cascading sponsored by Twitter, Etsy, eBay, Climate, Square, etc.—such as Scalding and Cascalog—which help integrate with a variety of different frameworks.

Scalding @Twitter

It's no wonder that Scala and Clojure have become the most popular languages used for commercial Cascading deployments. These languages are relatively flexible and dynamic for developers to use. Both include REPLs for interactive development, and both leverage functional programming. Yet they produce apps that tend toward the "conservatism" end of the spectrum, according to Yegge's argument.

Scalding provides a pipe abstraction that is easy to understand. Scalding and Scala in general have excellent features for developing large-scale data services. Cascalog apps are built from logical predicates—functions that represent queries, which in turn act much like unit tests. Software engineering practices for TDD, fault-tolerant workflows, etc., become simple to use at very large scale.

As a case in point, the revenue quality team at Twitter is quite different from Eric Ries's *Lean Startup* notion. The "lean" approach of pivoting toward initial customer adoption is great for start-ups, and potentially for larger organizations as well. However, initial customer adoption is not exactly an existential crisis for a large, popular social network. Instead they work with data at immense scale and complexity, with a mission to monetize social interactions among a very large, highly active community. Outages of the mission-critical apps that power Twitter's advertising servers would pose substantial risks to the business.

This team has standardized on Scalding for their apps. They've also written extensions, such as the Matrix API for very large-scale work in linear algebra and machine learning, so that complex apps can be expressed in a minimal amount of Scala code. All the while, those apps leverage the tooling that comes along with JVM use in large clusters, and conforms to Enterprise-scale requirements from Ops.

Using Code Examples

Most of the code samples in this book draw from the GitHub repository for Cascading:

- *https://github.com/Cascading*

We also show code based on these third-party GitHub repositories:

- *https://github.com/nathanmarz/cascalog*
- *https://github.com/twitter/scalding*

Safari® Books Online

 *Safari Books Online* is an on-demand digital library that delivers expert content in both book and video form from the world's leading authors in technology and business.

Technology professionals, software developers, web designers, and business and creative professionals use Safari Books Online as their primary resource for research, problem solving, learning, and certification training.

Safari Books Online offers a range of product mixes and pricing programs for organizations, government agencies, and individuals. Subscribers have access to thousands of books, training videos, and prepublication manuscripts in one fully searchable database from publishers like O'Reilly Media, Prentice Hall Professional, Addison-Wesley Professional, Microsoft Press, Sams, Que, Peachpit Press, Focal Press, Cisco Press, John Wiley & Sons, Syngress, Morgan Kaufmann, IBM Redbooks, Packt, Adobe Press, FT Press, Apress, Manning, New Riders, McGraw-Hill, Jones & Bartlett, Course Technology, and dozens more. For more information about Safari Books Online, please visit us online.

How to Contact Us

Please address comments and questions concerning this book to the publisher:

O'Reilly Media, Inc.
1005 Gravenstein Highway North
Sebastopol, CA 95472
800-998-9938 (in the United States or Canada)
707-829-0515 (international or local)
707-829-0104 (fax)

We have a web page for this book, where we list errata, examples, and any additional information. You can access this page at *http://oreil.ly/enterprise-data-workflows*.

To comment or ask technical questions about this book, send email to *bookques tions@oreilly.com*.

For more information about our books, courses, conferences, and news, see our website at *http://www.oreilly.com*.

Find us on Facebook: *http://facebook.com/oreilly*

Follow us on Twitter: *http://twitter.com/oreillymedia*

Watch us on YouTube: *http://www.youtube.com/oreillymedia*

Kudos

Many thanks go to Courtney Nash and Mike Loukides at O'Reilly; to Chris Wensel, author of Cascading, and other colleagues: Joe Posner, Gary Nakamura, Bill Wathen, Chris Nardi, Lisa Henderson, Arvind Jain, and Anthony Bull; to Chris Severs at eBay, and Dean Wampler for help with Scalding; to Girish Kathalagiri at AgilOne, and Vijay Srinivas Agneeswaran at Impetus for contributions to Pattern; to Serguey Boldyrev at Nokia, Stuart Evans at CMU, Julian Hyde at Optiq, Costin Leau at ElasticSearch, Viswa Sharma at TCS, Boris Chen, Donna Kidwell, and Jason Levitt for many suggestions and excellent feedback; to Hans Dockter at Gradleware for help with Gradle build scripts; to other contributors on the "Impatient" series (*http://bit.ly/1aVGkV4*) of code examples: Ken Krugler, Paul Lam, Stephane Landelle, Sujit Pal, Dmitry Ryaboy, Chris Severs, Branky Shao, and Matt Winkler; and to friends who provided invaluable help as technical reviewers for the early drafts: Paul Baclace, Bahman Bahmani, Manish Bhatt, Allen Day, Thomas Lockney, Joe Posner, Alex Robbins, Amit Sharma, Roy Seto, Branky Shao, Marcio Silva, James Todd, and Bill Worzel.

## CHAPTER 1

Getting Started

Programming Environment Setup

The following code examples show how to write apps in Cascading. The apps are intended to run on a laptop using Apache Hadoop in standalone mode, on a laptop running Linux or Unix (including Mac OS X). If you are using a Windows-based laptop, then many of these examples will not work, and generally speaking Hadoop does not behave well under Cygwin. However, you could run Linux, etc., in a virtual machine. Also, these examples are not intended to show how to set up and run a Hadoop cluster. There are other good resources about that—see *Hadoop: The Definitive Guide* (*http://hadoopbook.com/*) by Tom White (O'Reilly).

First, you will need to have a few platforms and tools installed:

Java (http://www.java.com/getjava/)
- Version 1.6.x was used to create these examples.
- Get the JDK, not the JRE.
- Install according to vendor instructions.

Apache Hadoop (http://hadoop.apache.org/)
- Version 1.0.x is needed for Cascading 2.x used in these examples.
- Be sure to install for "Standalone Operation."

Gradle (http://www.gradle.org/downloads)
- Version 1.3 or later is required for some examples in this book.
- Install according to vendor instructions.

Git (http://git-scm.com/)

- There are other ways to get code, but these examples show use of Git.

- Install according to vendor instructions.

Our use of Gradle and Git implies that these commands will be downloading JARs, checking code repos, etc., so you will need an Internet connection for most of the examples in this book.

Next, set up your command-line environment. You will need to have the following environment variables set properly, according to the installation instructions for each project and depending on your operating system:

- JAVA_HOME

- HADOOP_HOME

- GRADLE_HOME

Assuming that the installers for both Java and Git have placed binaries in the appropriate directories, now extend your PATH definition for the other tools that depend on Java:

```
$ export PATH=$PATH:$HADOOP_HOME/bin:$GRADLE_HOME/bin
```

OK, now for some tests. Try the following command lines to verify that your installations worked:

```
$ java -version
$ hadoop -version
$ gradle --version
$ git --version
```

Each command should print its version information. If there are problems, most likely you'll get errors at this stage. Don't worry if you see a warning like the following—that is a known behavior in Apache Hadoop:

```
Warning: $HADOOP_HOME is deprecated.
```

It's a great idea to create an account on GitHub (*http://github.com/*), too. An account is not required to run the sample apps in this book. However, it will help you follow project updates for the example code, participate within the developer community, ask questions, etc.

Also note that you do not need to install Cascading. Certainly you can, but the Gradle build scripts used in these examples will pull the appropriate version of Cascading from the Conjars Maven repo (*http://conjars.org/*) automatically. Conjars has lots of interesting JARs for related projects—take a peek sometime.

OK, now you are ready to download source code. Connect to a directory on your computer where you have a few gigabytes of available disk space, and then clone the whole source code repo for this multipart series:

```
$ git clone git://github.com/Cascading/Impatient.git
```

Once that completes, connect into the *part1* subdirectory. You're ready to begin programming in Cascading.

Example 1: Simplest Possible App in Cascading

The first item on our agenda is how to write a simple Cascading app (*http://www.cascad ing.org/*). The goal is clear and concise: create the simplest possible app in Cascading while following best practices. This app will copy a file, potentially a very large file, in parallel—in other words, it performs a distributed copy. No bangs, no whistles, just good solid code.

First, we create a source tap to specify the input data. That data happens to be formatted as tab-separated values (TSV) with a header row, which the TextDelimited (*http://bit.ly/ 165Pyqz*) data scheme handles.

```
String inPath = args[ 0 ];
Tap inTap = new Hfs( new TextDelimited( true, "\t" ), inPath );
```

Next we create a sink tap to specify the output data, which will also be in TSV format:

```
String outPath = args[ 1 ];
Tap outTap = new Hfs( new TextDelimited( true, "\t" ), outPath );
```

Then we create a pipe to connect the taps:

```
Pipe copyPipe = new Pipe( "copy" );
```

Here comes the fun part. Get your tool belt ready, because we need to do a little plumbing. Connect the taps and the pipe to create a flow:

```
FlowDef flowDef = FlowDef.flowDef()
 .addSource( copyPipe, inTap )
 .addTailSink( copyPipe, outTap );
```

The notion of a workflow (*http://en.wikipedia.org/wiki/Workflow*) lives at the heart of Cascading. Instead of thinking in terms of map and reduce phases in a Hadoop job step, Cascading developers define workflows and business processes as if they were doing plumbing work.

Enterprise data workflows tend to use lots of job steps. Those job steps are connected and have dependencies, specified as a directed acyclic graph (DAG) (*http://bit.ly/ 17JpxAL*). Cascading uses FlowDef objects (*http://bit.ly/11gRYXk*) to define how a flow—that is to say, a portion of the DAG—must be connected. A pipe must connect to both a source and a sink. Done and done. That defines the simplest flow possible.

Now that we have a flow defined, one last line of code invokes the planner on it. Planning a flow is akin to the physical plan for a query in SQL. The planner verifies that the correct fields are available for each operation, that the sequence of operations makes sense, and that all of the pipes and taps are connected in some meaningful way. If the planner detects any problems, it will throw exceptions long before the app gets submitted to the Hadoop cluster.

```
flowConnector.connect( flowDef ).complete();
```

Generally, these Cascading source lines go into a static `main` method in a `Main` class. Look in the *part1/src/main/java/impatient/* directory, in the *Main.java* file, where this is already done. You should be good to go.

Each different kind of computing framework is called a *topology*, and each must have its own planner class. This example code uses the `HadoopFlowConnector` class to invoke the flow planner, which generates the Hadoop job steps needed to implement the flow. Cascading performs that work on the client side, and then submits those jobs to the Hadoop cluster and tracks their status.

If you want to read in more detail about the classes in the Cascading API that were used, see the Cascading *User Guide* and *JavaDoc* (*http://www.cascading.org/documentation/*).

Build and Run

Cascading uses Gradle to build the JAR for an app. The build script for "Example 1: Simplest Possible App in Cascading" is in *build.gradle*:

```
apply plugin: 'java'
apply plugin: 'idea'
apply plugin: 'eclipse'

archivesBaseName = 'impatient'

repositories {
  mavenLocal()
  mavenCentral()
  mavenRepo name: 'conjars', url: 'http://conjars.org/repo/'
}

ext.cascadingVersion = '2.1.0'

dependencies {
  compile( group: 'cascading', name: 'cascading-core', version: cascadingVersion )
  compile( group: 'cascading', name: 'cascading-hadoop', version: cascadingVersion )
}

jar {
  description = "Assembles a Hadoop ready jar file"
  doFirst {
```

```
    into( 'lib' ) {
      from configurations.compile
    }
  }

  manifest {
    attributes( "Main-Class": "impatient/Main" )
  }
}
```

Notice the reference to a Maven repo called `http://conjars.org/repo/` in the build script. That is how Gradle accesses the appropriate version of Cascading, pulling from the open source project's *Conjars* public Maven repo.

Books about Gradle and Maven

For more information about using Gradle and Maven, check out these books:

- *Building and Testing with Gradle: Understanding Next-Generation Builds* by Tim Berglund and Matthew McCullough (O'Reilly)
- *Maven: The Definitive Guide* by Sonatype Company (O'Reilly)

To build this sample app from a command line, run Gradle:

```
$ gradle clean jar
```

Note that each Cascading app gets compiled into a single JAR file. That is to say, it includes all of the app's business logic, system integrations, unit tests, assertions, exception handling, etc. The principle is "Same JAR, any scale." After building a Cascading app as a JAR, a developer typically runs it on a laptop for unit tests and other validation using relatively small-scale data. Once those tests are confirmed, the JAR typically moves into continuous integration (CI) (*http://bit.ly/12GYaBK*) on a staging cluster using moderate-scale data. After passing CI, Enterprise IT environments generally place a tested JAR into a Maven repository as a new version of the app that Ops will schedule for production use with the full data sets.

What you should have at this point is a JAR file that is ready to run. Before running it, be sure to clear the *output* directory. Apache Hadoop insists on this when you're running in standalone mode. To be clear, these examples are working with input and output paths that are in the local filesystem, not HDFS.

Now run the app:

```
$ rm -rf output
$ hadoop jar ./build/libs/impatient.jar data/rain.txt output/rain
```

Notice how those command-line arguments (actual parameters) align with the `args[]` array (formal parameters) in the source. In the first argument, the source tap loads from the input file *data/rain.txt*, which contains text from search results about "rain shadow." Each line is supposed to represent a different document. The first two lines look like this:

```
doc_id  text
doc01   A rain shadow is a dry area on the lee back side of a mountainous area.
```

Input tuples get copied, TSV row by TSV row, to the sink tap. The second argument specifies that the sink tap be written to the `output/rain` output, which is organized as a partition file. You can verify that those lines got copied by viewing the text output, for example:

```
$ head -2 output/rain/part-00000
doc_id  text
doc01   A rain shadow is a dry area on the lee back side of a mountainous area.
```

For quick reference, the source code, input data, and a log for this example are listed in a GitHub gist (*https://gist.github.com/2911686*). If the log of your run looks terribly different, something is probably not set up correctly. There are multiple ways to interact with the Cascading developer community. You can post a note on the `cascading-user` email forum (*http://bit.ly/19U7Lvl*). Plenty of experienced Cascading users are discussing taps and pipes and flows there, and they are eager to help. Or you can visit one of the Cascading user group meetings (*http://www.meetup.com/cascading/*).

Cascading Taxonomy

Conceptually, a "flow diagram" for this first example is shown in Figure 1-1. Our simplest app possible copies lines of text from file "A" to file "B." The "M" and "R" labels represent the map and reduce phases, respectively. As the flow diagram shows, it uses one job step in Apache Hadoop: only one map and no reduce needed. The implementation is a brief Java program, 10 lines long.

Wait—10 lines of code to copy a file? That seems excessive; certainly this same work could be performed in much quicker ways, such as using the `cp` command on Linux. However, keep in mind that Cascading is about the "plumbing" required to make Enterprise apps robust. There is some overhead in the setup, but those lines of code won't change much as an app's complexity grows. That overhead helps provide for the principle of "Same JAR, any scale."

Let's take a look at the components of a Cascading app. Figure 1-2 shows a taxonomy that starts with *apps* at the top level. An app has a unique signature and is versioned, and it includes one or more *flows*. Optionally, those flows may be organized into *cascades*, which are collections of flows without dependencies on one another, so that they may be run in parallel.

Each flow represents a physical plan, based on the planner for a specific topology such as Apache Hadoop. The physical plan provides a deterministic strategy for a query. Developers talk about a principle of "Fail the same way twice." In other words, when we need to debug an issue, it's quite important that Cascading flows behave deterministically. Otherwise, the process of troubleshooting edge cases on a large cluster and with a large data set can become enormous. Again, that addresses a more "conservatism" aspect of Cascading.

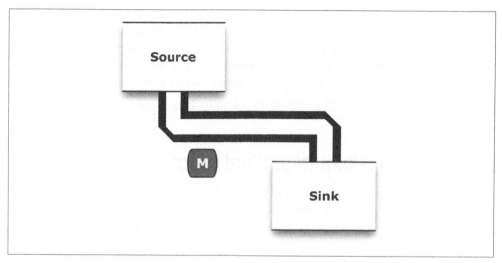

Figure 1-1. Flow diagram for "Example 1: Simplest Possible App in Cascading"

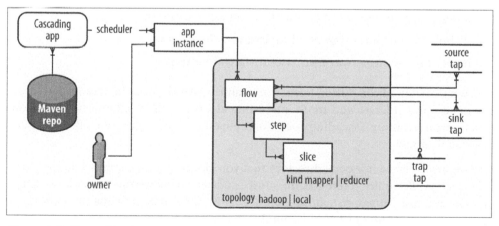

Figure 1-2. Cascading taxonomy

We've already introduced the use of pipes. Each assembly of pipes has a head and a tail. We bind taps to pipes to create a flow; so *source taps* get bound to the heads of pipes for input data, and *sink taps* to the tails of pipes for output data. That is the functional graph. Any unconnected pipes and taps will cause the planner to throw exceptions.

The physical plan of a flow results in a dependency graph of one or more *steps*. Formally speaking, that is a directed acyclic graph (DAG). At runtime, data flows through the DAG as streams of key/value *tuples*.

The steps created by a Hadoop flow planner, for example, correspond to the job steps that run on the Hadoop cluster. Within each step there may be multiple phases, e.g., the map phase or reduce phase in Hadoop. Also, each step is composed of *slices*. These are the most granular "unit of work" in a Cascading app, such that collections of slices can be parallelized. In Hadoop these slices correspond to the tasks executing in task slots.

That's it in a nutshell, how the proverbial neck bone gets connected to the collarbone in Cascading.

Example 2: The Ubiquitous Word Count

The first example showed how to do a file copy in Cascading. Let's take that code and stretch it a bit further. Undoubtedly you've seen Word Count (*http://en.wikipedia.org/ wiki/Word_count*) before. We'd feel remiss if we did not provide an example.

Word Count serves as a "Hello World" for Hadoop apps. In other words, this simple program provides a great test case for parallel processing:

- It requires a minimal amount of code.
- It demonstrates use of both symbolic and numeric values.
- It shows a dependency graph of tuples as an abstraction.
- It is not many steps away from useful search indexing.

When a distributed computing framework can run Word Count in parallel at scale, it can handle much larger and more interesting algorithms. Along the way, we'll show how to use a few more Cascading operations, plus show how to generate a flow diagram as a visualization.

Starting from the source code directory that you cloned in Git, connect into the *part2* subdirectory. For quick reference, the source code and a log for this example are listed in a GitHub gist (*https://gist.github.com/3020297*). Input data remains the same as in the earlier code (*https://gist.github.com/2911686*).

Note that the names of the taps have changed. Instead of `inTap` and `outTap`, we're using `docTap` and `wcTap` now. We'll be adding more taps, so this will help us have more descriptive names. This makes it simpler to follow all the plumbing.

Previously we defined a simple pipe to connect the taps. This example shows a more complex *pipe assembly*. We use a generator inside an Each (*http://bit.ly/10zIVyc*) to split the document text into a token stream. The generator uses a regex to split the input text on word boundaries:

```
Fields token = new Fields( "token" );
Fields text = new Fields( "text" );
RegexSplitGenerator splitter
  = new RegexSplitGenerator( token, "[ \\[\\]\\(\\)),.]" );
// returns only "token"
Pipe docPipe = new Each( "token", text, splitter, Fields.RESULTS );
```

Out of that pipe, we get a tuple stream of token values. One benefit of using a regex is that it's simple to change. We can handle more complex cases of splitting tokens without having to rewrite the generator.

Next, we use a GroupBy (*http://bit.ly/120VnrN*) to count the occurrences of each token:

```
Pipe wcPipe = new Pipe( "wc", docPipe );
wcPipe = new GroupBy( wcPipe, token );
wcPipe = new Every( wcPipe, Fields.ALL, new Count(), Fields.ALL );
```

Notice that we've used Each and Every to perform operations within the pipe assembly. The difference between these two is that an Each operates on individual tuples so that it takes Function operations. An Every operates on groups of tuples so that it takes Aggregator or Buffer operations—in this case the GroupBy performed an aggregation. The different ways of inserting operations serve to categorize the different built-in operations in Cascading. They also illustrate how the pattern language syntax guides the development of workflows.

From that wcPipe we get a resulting tuple stream of token and count for the output. Again, we connect the plumbing with a FlowDef (*http://bit.ly/11gRYXk*):

```
FlowDef flowDef = FlowDef.flowDef()
  .setName( "wc" )
  .addSource( docPipe, docTap )
  .addTailSink( wcPipe, wcTap );
```

Finally, we generate a DOT file (*http://en.wikipedia.org/wiki/DOT_language*) to depict the Cascading flow graphically. You can load the DOT file into OmniGraffle (*https://www.omnigroup.com/products/omnigraffle/*) or Visio. Those diagrams are really helpful for troubleshooting workflows in Cascading:

```
Flow wcFlow = flowConnector.connect( flowDef );
wcFlow.writeDOT( "dot/wc.dot" );
wcFlow.complete();
```

This code is already in the *part2/src/main/java/impatient/* directory, in the *Main.java* file. To build it:

```
$ gradle clean jar
```

Then to run it:

```
$ rm -rf output
$ hadoop jar ./build/libs/impatient.jar data/rain.txt output/wc
```

This second example uses the same input from the first example, but we expect different output. The sink tap writes to the partition file *output/wc*, and the first 10 lines (including a header) should look like this:

```
$ head output/wc/part-00000
token          count
               9
A              3
Australia      1
Broken         1
California's   1
DVD            1
Death          1
Land           1
Secrets        1
```

Again, a GitHub gist (*https://gist.github.com/3020297*) shows building and running the sample app. If your run looks terribly different, something is probably not set up correctly. Ask the Cascading developer community how to troubleshoot for your environment.

So that's our Word Count example. Eighteen lines of yummy goodness.

Flow Diagrams

Conceptually, we can examine a workflow as a stylized flow diagram. This helps visualize the "plumbing" metaphor by using a design that removes low-level details. Figure 1-3 shows one of these for "Example 2: The Ubiquitous Word Count". Formally speaking, this diagram represents a DAG.

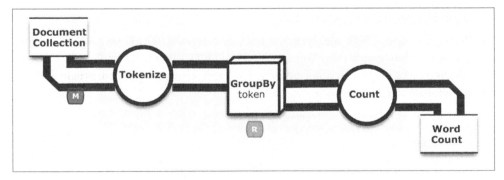

Figure 1-3. Conceptual flow diagram for "Example 2: The Ubiquitous Word Count"

Meanwhile the Cascading code in "Example 2: The Ubiquitous Word Count" writes a *flow diagram* called *dot/wc.dot* to depict the flow graphically. Figure 1-4 shows a version that has been annotated to indicate where the map and reduce phases run. As mentioned before, those diagrams come in handy when troubleshooting Cascading workflows. If you ask other Cascading developers for help debugging an issue, don't be surprised when their first request is to see your app's flow diagram.

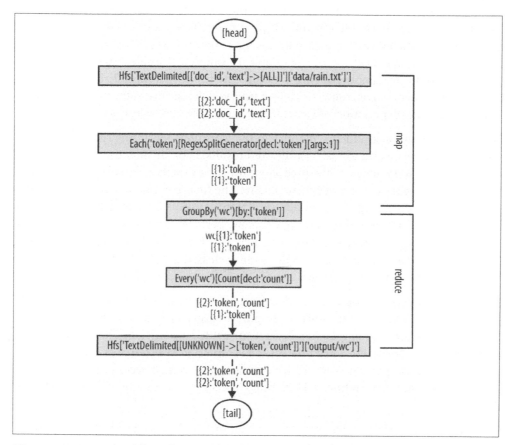

Figure 1-4. Annotated flow diagram for "Example 2: The Ubiquitous Word Count"

From a high-level perspective, "Example 2: The Ubiquitous Word Count" differs from "Example 1: Simplest Possible App in Cascading" in two ways:

- Source and sink taps are more specific.
- Three operators have been added to the pipe assembly.

Although several lines of Java source code changed, in pattern language terms we can express the difference between the apps simply as those two points. That's a powerful benefit of using the "plumbing" metaphor.

First let's consider how the source and sink taps were redefined to be more specific. Instead of simply describing a generic "Source" or "File A," now we've defined the source tap as a collection of text documents. Instead of "Sink" or "File B," now we've defined the sink tap to produce word count tuples—the desired end result. Those changes in the taps began to reference fields in the tuple stream. The source tap in both examples was based on `TextDelimited` with parameters so that it reads a TSV file and uses the header line to assign field names. "Example 1: Simplest Possible App in Cascading" ignored the fields by simply copying data tuple by tuple. "Example 2: The Ubiquitous Word Count" begins to reference fields by name, which introduces the notion of *scheme* —imposing some expectation of structure on otherwise unstructured data.

The change in taps also added semantics to the workflow, specifying requirements for added operations needed to reach the desired results. Let's consider the new Cascading operations that were added to the pipe assembly in "Example 1: Simplest Possible App in Cascading": `Tokenize`, `GroupBy`, and `Count`. The first one, `Tokenize`, transforms the input data tuples, splitting lines of text into a stream of tokens. That transform represents the "T" in ETL. The second operation, `GroupBy`, performs an aggregation. In terms of Hadoop, this causes a reduce with `token` as a key. The third operation, `Count`, gets applied to each aggregation—counting the values for each `token` key, i.e., the number of instances of each token in the stream.

The deltas between "Example 1: Simplest Possible App in Cascading" and "Example 2: The Ubiquitous Word Count" illustrate important aspects of Cascading. Consider how data tuples flow through a pipe assembly, getting routed through familiar data operators such as `GroupBy`, `Count`, etc. Each flow must be connected to a source of data as its input and a sink as its output. The sink tap for one flow may in turn become a source tap for another flow. Each flow defines a DAG that Cascading uses to infer schema from unstructured data.

Enterprise data workflows are complex applications, and managing that complexity is the purpose for Cascading. Enterprise apps based on Apache Hadoop typically involve more than just one Hadoop job step. Some apps are known to include hundreds of job steps, with complex dependencies between them. Cascading leverages this concept of a DAG to represent the business process of an app. The DAG, in turn, declares the requirements for the job steps that are needed to complete the app's data flow. Consequently, a flow planner has sufficient information about the workflow so that it can leverage the DAG in several ways:

- Ensure that necessary fields are available to operations that require them—based on tuple scheme.

- Apply transformations to help optimize the app—e.g., moving code from reduce into map.

- Track data provenance across different sources and sinks—understand the producer/consumer relationship of data products.

- Annotate the DAG with metrics from each step, across the history of an app's instances—capacity planning, notifications for data drops, etc.

- Identify or predict bottlenecks, e.g., key/value skew as the shape of the input data changes—troubleshoot apps.

Those capabilities address important concerns in Enterprise IT and stand as key points by which Cascading differentiates itself from other Hadoop abstraction layers.

Another subtle point concerns the use of *taps*. On one hand, data taps are available for integrating Cascading with several other popular data frameworks, including Memcached, HBase, Cassandra, etc. Several popular data serialization systems are supported, such as Apache Thrift, Avro, Kyro, etc. Looking at the conceptual flow diagram, our workflow could be using any of a variety of different data frameworks and serialization systems. That could apply equally well to SQL query result sets via JDBC or to data coming from Cassandra via Thrift. It wouldn't be difficult to modify the code in "Example 2: The Ubiquitous Word Count" to set those details based on configuration parameters. To wit, the taps generalize many physical aspects of the data so that we can leverage patterns.

On the other hand, taps also help manage complexity at scale. Our code in "Example 2: The Ubiquitous Word Count" could be run on a laptop in Hadoop's "standalone" mode to process a small file such as *rain.txt*, which is a mere 510 bytes. The same code could be run on a 1,000-node Hadoop cluster to process several petabytes of the Internet Archives' Wayback Machine (*http://archive.org/web/web.php*).

Taps are agnostic about scale, because the underlying topology (Hadoop) uses parallelism to handle very large data. Generally speaking, Cascading apps handle scale-out into larger and larger data sets by changing the parameters used to define taps. Taps themselves are *formal parameters* that specify placeholders for input and output data. When a Cascading app runs, its *actual parameters* specify the actual data to be used—whether those are HDFS partition files, HBase data objects, Memcached key/values, etc. We call these *tap identifiers*. They are effectively *uniform resource identifiers* (URIs) for connecting through protocols such as HDFS, JDBC, etc. A dependency graph of tap identifiers and the history of app instances that produced or consumed them is analogous to a *catalog* in relational databases.

Predictability at Scale

The code in "Example 1: Simplest Possible App in Cascading" showed how to move data from point A to point B. That was simply a distributed file copy—loading data via distributed tasks, or the "L" in ETL.

A copy example may seem trivial, and it may seem like Cascading is overkill for that. However, moving important data from point A to point B reliably can be a crucial job to perform. This helps illustrate one of the key reasons to use Cascading.

Consider an analogy of building a small Ferris wheel. With a little bit of imagination and some background in welding, a person could cobble one together using old bicycle parts. In fact, those DIY Ferris wheels show up at events such as Maker Faire (*http://makerfaire.com/*). Starting out, a person might construct a little Ferris wheel, just for demo. It might not hold anything larger than hamsters, but it's not a hard problem. With a bit more skill, a person could probably build a somewhat larger instance, one that's big enough for small children to ride.

Ask yourself this: how robust would a DIY Ferris wheel need to be before you let your kids ride on it? That's precisely part of the challenge at an event like Maker Faire. Makers must be able to build a device such as a Ferris wheel out of spare bicycle parts that is robust enough that strangers will let their kids ride. Let's hope those welds were made using best practices and good materials, to avoid catastrophes.

That's a key reason why Cascading was created. When you need to move a few gigabytes from point A to point B, it's probably simple enough to write a Bash script, or just use a single command-line copy. When your work requires some reshaping of the data, then a few lines of Python will probably work fine. Run that Python code from your Bash script and you're done.

That's a great approach, when it fits the use case requirements. However, suppose you're not moving just gigabytes. Suppose you're moving terabytes, or petabytes. Bash scripts won't get you very far. Also think about this: suppose an app not only needs to move data from point A to point B, but it must follow the required best practices of an Enterprise IT shop. Millions of dollars and potentially even some jobs ride on the fact that the app performs correctly. Day in and day out. That's not unlike trusting a Ferris wheel made by strangers; the users want to make sure it wasn't just built out of spare bicycle parts by some amateur welder. Robustness is key.

Or, taking this analogy a few steps in another interesting direction, perhaps you're not only moving data and reshaping it a little, but you're applying some interesting machine learning algorithms, some natural language processing, gene sequencing…who knows? Those imply lots of resource use, lots of potential expense in case of failures. Or lots of customer exposure. You'll want to use an application framework that is significantly more robust than a bunch of scripts cobbled together.

With Cascading, you can package your entire MapReduce application, including its orchestration and testing, within a single JAR file. You define all of that within the context of one programming language—whether that language may be Java, Scala, Clojure, Python, Ruby, etc. That way your tests are included within a single program, not spread across several scripts written in different languages. Having a single JAR file define an app helps for following the best practices required in Enterprise IT: unit tests, stream assertions, revision control, continuous integration, Maven repos, role-based configuration management, advanced schedulers, monitoring and notifications, data provenance, etc. Those are key reasons why we make Cascading, and why people use it for robust apps that run at scale.

## CHAPTER 2

Extending Pipe Assemblies

Example 3: Customized Operations

Cascading provides a wide range of built-in operations (*http://bit.ly/19Y18eR*) to perform on workflows. For many apps, the Cascading API is more than sufficient. However, you may run into cases where a slightly different transformation is needed. Each of the Cascading operations can be extended by subclassing in Java. Let's extend the Cascading app from "Example 2: The Ubiquitous Word Count" on page 8 to show how to customize an operation.

Modifying a conceptual flow diagram is a good way to add new requirements for a Cascading app. Figure 2-1 shows how this iteration of Word Count can be modified to clean up the token stream. A new class for this example will go right after the Token ize operation so that it can scrub each tuple. In terms of Cascading patterns, this operation needs to be used in an Each operator, so we must implement it as a Function.

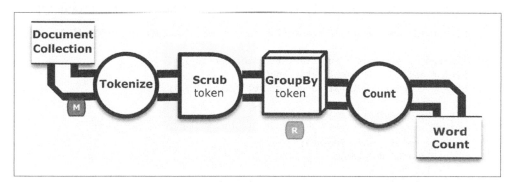

Figure 2-1. Conceptual flow diagram for "Example 3: Customized Operations"

Starting from the source code directory that you cloned in Git, connect into the *part3* subdirectory. We'll define a new class called `ScrubFunction` as our custom operation, which subclasses from BaseOperation (*http://bit.ly/19Y18eR*) while implementing the Function (*http://bit.ly/19Y18eR*) interface:

```
public class ScrubFunction extends BaseOperation implements Function { ... }
```

Next, we need to define a constructor, which specifies how this function consumes from the tuple stream:

```
public ScrubFunction( Fields fieldDeclaration )
  {
  super( 2, fieldDeclaration );
  }
```

The `fieldDeclaration` parameter declares a list of fields that will be consumed from the tuple stream. Based on the intended use, we know that the tuple stream will have two fields at that point, doc_id and token. We can constrain this class to allow exactly two fields as the number of arguments. Great, now we know what the new operation expects as arguments.

Next we define a `scrubText` method to clean up tokens. The following is the business logic of the function:

```
public String scrubText( String text )
  {
  return text.trim().toLowerCase();
  }
```

This version is relatively simple. In production it would typically have many more cases handled. Having the business logic defined as a separate method makes it simpler to write unit tests against.

Next, we define an `operate` method. This is essentially a wrapper that takes an argument tuple, applies our `scrubText` method to each token, and then produces a result tuple:

```
public void operate( FlowProcess flowProcess, FunctionCall functionCall )
  {
  TupleEntry argument = functionCall.getArguments();
  String doc_id = argument.getString( 0 );
  String token = scrubText( argument.getString( 1 ) );

  if( token.length() > 0 )
    {
    Tuple result = new Tuple();
    result.add( doc_id );
    result.add( token );
    functionCall.getOutputCollector().add( result );
    }
  }
```

Let's consider the context of a function within a pipe assembly, as shown in Figure 2-2. At runtime, a pipe assembly takes an input stream of tuples and produces an output stream of tuples.

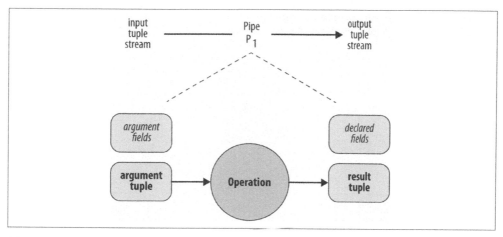

Figure 2-2. Pipe assembly

Note that by inserting an operation, we must add another pipe. Pipes get connected together in this way to produce pipe assemblies. Looking into this in more detail, as Figure 2-2 shows, an operation takes an argument tuple—one tuple at a time—and produces a result tuple. Each argument tuple from the input stream must fit the argument fields defined in the operation class. Similarly, each result tuple going to the output stream must fit the declared fields.

Now let's place this new class into a *ScrubFunction.java* source file. Then we need to change the docPipe pipe assembly to insert our custom operation immediately after the tokenizer:

```
Fields scrubArguments = new Fields( "doc_id", "token" );
ScrubFunction scrubFunc = new ScrubFunction( scrubArguments );
docPipe = new Each( docPipe, scrubArguments, scrubFunc, Fields.RESULTS );
```

Notice how the doc_id and token fields are defined in the scrubArguments parameter. That matches what we specified in the constructor. Also, note how the Each operator uses Field.RESULTS as its field selector. In other words, this tells the pipe to discard argument tuple values (from the input stream) and instead use only the result tuple values (for the output stream).

Figure 2-3 shows how an Each operator inserts a Function into a pipe. In this case, the new customized ScrubFunction is fitted between two pipes, both of which are named docPipe. That's another important point: pipes have names, and they inherit names from where they connect—until something changes, such as a join. The name stays the same up until just before the GroupBy aggregation:

```
// determine the word counts
Pipe wcPipe = new Pipe( "wc", docPipe );
wcPipe = new Retain( wcPipe, token );
wcPipe = new GroupBy( wcPipe, token );
```

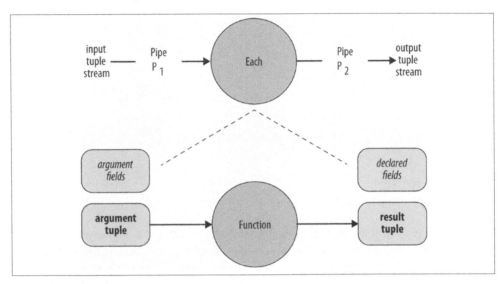

Figure 2-3. Each with a function

Then we create a new pipe named wc and add a Retain (*http://bit.ly/14NXRbB*) subassembly. This discards all the fields in the tuple stream except for token, to help make the final output simpler. We put that just before the GroupBy to reduce the amount of work required in the aggregation.

Look in the *part3/src/main/java/impatient/* directory, where the *Main.java* and *Scrub-Function.java* source files have already been modified. You should be good to go.

To build:

```
$ gradle clean jar
```

To run:

```
$ rm -rf output
$ hadoop jar ./build/libs/impatient.jar data/rain.txt output/wc
```

This uses the same input as the previous examples, but we expect slightly different output due to the token scrubbing. In the output, the first 10 lines (including the header) should look like this:

```
$ more output/wc/part-00000
token           count
a               8
air             1
an              1
and             2
area            4
as              2
australia       1
back            1
broken          1
```

A gist on GitHub (*https://gist.github.com/3021655*) shows building and running "Example 3: Customized Operations". If your run looks terribly different, something is probably not set up correctly. Ask the developer community for advice.

Scrubbing Tokens

Previously in "Example 2: The Ubiquitous Word Count" we used a RegexSplitGenerator (*http://bit.ly/15gchmK*) to tokenize the text. That built-in operation works quite well for many use cases. "Example 3: Customized Operations" used a custom operation in Cascading to "scrub" the token stream prior to counting the tokens. It's important to understand the trade-offs between these two approaches. When should you leverage the existing API, versus extending it?

One thing you'll find in working with almost any text analytics (*http://en.wikipedia.org/ wiki/Text_analytics*) at scale is that there are lots of edge cases. Cleaning up edge cases —character sets, inconsistent hyphens, different kinds of quotes, exponents, etc.—is usually the bulk of engineering work. If you try to incorporate every possible variation into a regex, you end up with code that is both brittle and difficult to understand, especially when you hit another rare condition six months later and must go back and reread your (long-forgotten) complex regex notation.

Identifying edge cases for text analytics at scale is an iterative process, based on learnings over time, based on experiences with the data. Some edge cases might be encountered only after processing orders of magnitude more data than the initial test cases. Also, each application tends to have its own nuances. That makes it difficult to use "off the shelf" libraries for text processing in large-scale production.

So in "Example 3: Customized Operations" we showed how to extend Cascading by subclassing BaseOperation to write our own "scrubber." One benefit is that we can handle many edge cases, adding more as they become identified. Better yet, in terms of separation of concerns, we can add new edge cases as unit tests for our custom class, then code to them. More about unit tests later.

For now, a key point is that customized operations in Cascading are not *user-defined functions* (UDFs). Customized operations get defined in the same language as the rest of the app, so the compiler is aware of all code being added. This extends the Cascading API by subclassing, so that the API contract must still be honored. Several benefits apply —which are the flip side of what a programmer encounters in Hive or Pig apps, where integration occurs outside the language of the app.

Operations act on the data to transform the tuple stream, filter it, analyze it, etc. Think about the roles that command-line utilities such as `grep` or `awk` perform in Linux shell scripts—instead of having to rewrite custom programs.

Similarly, Cascading provides a rich library of standard operations to codify the business logic of transforming Big Data. It's relatively simple to develop your own custom operations, as our text "scrubbing" in "Example 3: Customized Operations" shows. However, if you find yourself starting to develop lots of custom operations every time you begin to write a Cascading app, that's an *anti-pattern*. In other words, it's a good indication that you should step back and reevaluate.

What is the risk in customizing the API components? That goes back to the notion of pattern language. On one hand, the standard operations in Cascading have been developed over a period of years. They tend to cover a large class of MapReduce applications already. The standard operations encapsulate best practices and design patterns for parallelism. On the other hand, if you aren't careful while defining a custom operation, you may inadvertently introduce a performance bottleneck. Something to think about.

Example 4: Replicated Joins

Let's build on our Word Count app to introduce the use of a join in Cascading. Joins at scale in Hadoop are a complex issue. We'll add a "stop words" list to our app, which takes advantage of the join and demonstrates a best practice about joins and preserving parallelism at scale. A conceptual flow diagram for this iteration of Word Count in Cascading is shown in Figure 2-4.

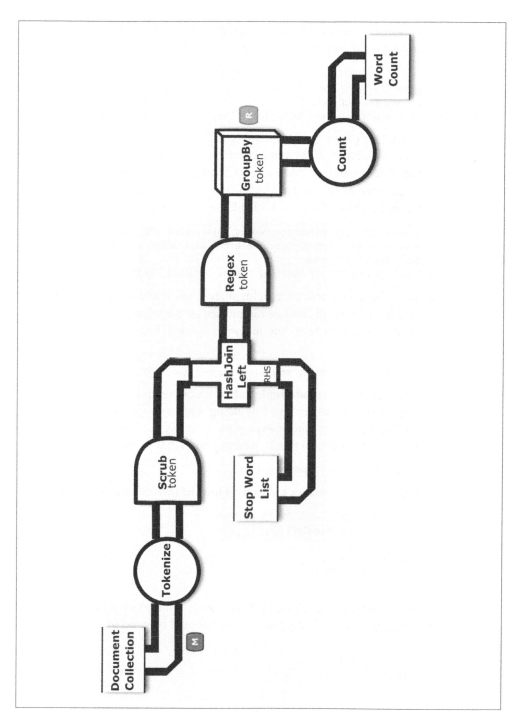

Figure 2-4. Conceptual flow diagram for "Example 4: Replicated Joins"

Starting from the source code directory that you cloned in Git, connect into the *part4* subdirectory. First let's add another source tap to read the stop words list as an input data set:

```
String stopPath = args[ 2 ];
Fields stop = new Fields( "stop" );
Tap stopTap = new Hfs( new TextDelimited( stop, true, "\t" ), stopPath );
```

Next we'll insert another pipe into the assembly to connect to the stop words source tap. Note that a join combines data from two or more pipes based on common field values. We call the pipes streaming into a join its *branches*. For the join in our example, the existing docPipe provides one branch, while the new stopPipe provides the other. Then we use a HashJoin (*http://bit.ly/14NXTQA*) to perform a left join:

```
// perform a left join to remove stop words, discarding the rows
// which joined with stop words, i.e., were non-null after left join
Pipe stopPipe = new Pipe( "stop" );
Pipe tokenPipe = new HashJoin( docPipe, token, stopPipe, stop, new LeftJoin() );
```

When the values of the token and stop fields match, the result tuple has a non-null value for stop. Then a stop word has been identified in the token stream. So next we discard all the non-null results from the left join, using a RegexFilter (*http://bit.ly/12m2G9G*):

```
tokenPipe = new Each( tokenPipe, stop, new RegexFilter( "^$" ) );
```

Tuples that match the given pattern are kept, and tuples that do not match get discarded. Therefore the stop words all get removed by using a left join with a filter. This new tokenPipe can be fitted back into the wcPipe pipe assembly that we had in earlier examples. The workflow continues on much the same from that point:

```
Pipe wcPipe = new Pipe( "wc", tokenPipe );
```

Last, we include the additional source tap to the FlowDef (*http://bit.ly/11gRYXk*):

```
// connect the taps, pipes, etc., into a flow
FlowDef flowDef = FlowDef.flowDef()
 .setName( "wc" )
 .addSource( docPipe, docTap )
 .addSource( stopPipe, stopTap )
 .addTailSink( wcPipe, wcTap );
```

Modify the Main method for these changes. This code is already in the *part4/src/main/java/impatient/* directory, in the *Main.java* file. You should be good to go.

To build:

```
$ gradle clean jar
```

To run:

```
$ rm -rf output
$ hadoop jar ./build/libs/impatient.jar data/rain.txt output/wc data/en.stop
```

Again, this uses the same input from "Example 1: Simplest Possible App in Cascading", but now we expect all stop words to be removed from the output stream. Common words such as a, an, as, etc., have been filtered out.

You can verify the entire output text in the *output/wc* partition file, where the first 10 lines (including the header) should look like this:

```
$ head output/wc/part-00000
token        count
air          1
area         4
australia    1
broken       1
california's 1
cause        1
cloudcover   1
death        1
deserts      1
```

The flow diagram will be in the *dot/* subdirectory after the app runs. For those keeping score, the resulting physical plan in Apache Hadoop uses one map and one reduce.

Again, a GitHub gist (*https://gist.github.com/3043745*) shows building and running this example. If your run looks terribly different, something is probably not set up correctly. Ask the developer community for advice.

Stop Words and Replicated Joins

Let's consider why we would want to use a stop words (*http://en.wikipedia.org/wiki/ Stop_words*) list. This approach originated in work by Hans Peter Luhn (*http://en.wiki pedia.org/wiki/Hans_Peter_Luhn*) at IBM Research, during the dawn of computing. The reasons for it are twofold. On one hand, consider that the most common words in any given natural language are generally not useful for text analytics (*http://en.wikipe dia.org/wiki/Text_analytics*). For example, in English, words such as "and," "of," and "the" are probably not what you want to search and probably not interesting for Word Count metrics. They represent high frequency and low semantic value within the token distribution. They also represent the bulk of the processing required. Natural languages tend to have on the order of 10^5 words, so the potential size of any stop words list is nicely bounded. Filtering those high-frequency words out of the token stream dramatically reduces the amount of processing required later in the workflow.

On the other hand, you may also want to remove some words explicitly from the token stream. This almost always comes up in practice, especially when working with public discussions such as social network comments.

Think about it: what are some of the most common words posted online in comments? Words that are not the most common words in "polite" English? Do you really want those words to bubble up in your text analytics? In automated systems that leverage unsupervised learning (*http://en.wikipedia.org/wiki/Unsupervised_learning*), this can lead to highly embarrassing situations. *Caveat machinator.*

Next, let's consider working with a Joiner (*http://bit.ly/13lOQur*) in Cascading. We have two pipes: one for the "scrubbed" token stream and another for the stop words list. We want to filter all instances of tokens from the stop words list out of the token stream. If we weren't working in MapReduce, a naive approach would be to load the stop words list into a hashtable, then iterate through our token stream to lookup each token in the hashtable and delete it if found. If we were coding in Hadoop directly, a less naive approach would be to put the stop words list into the distributed cache (*http://bit.ly/14R3pSq*) and have a job step that loads it during setup, then rinse/lather/repeat from the naive coding approach described earlier.

Instead we leverage the workflow orchestration in Cascading. One might write a custom operation, as we did in the previous example—e.g., a custom Filter (*http://bit.ly/1cRAyQJ*) that performs lookups on a list of stop words. That's extra work, and not particularly efficient in parallel anyway.

Cascading provides for joins on pipes, and conceptually a left outer join (*http://bit.ly/19TVqar*) solves our requirement to filter stop words. Think of joining the token stream with the stop words list. When the result is non-null, the join has identified a stop word. Discard it.

Understand that there's a big problem with using joins at scale in Hadoop. Outside of the context of a relational database (*http://bit.ly/18w60GV*), arbitrary joins do not perform well. Suppose you have N items in one tuple stream and M items in another and want to join them? In the general case, for an arbitrary join, that requires $N \times M$ operations and also introduces a data dependency (*http://bit.ly/14qS0Kh*), such that the join cannot be performed in parallel. If both N and M are relatively large, say in the millions of tuples, then we'd end up processing 10^{12} operations on a single processor—which defeats the purpose in terms of leveraging MapReduce.

Fortunately, if some of that data is sparse (*http://en.wikipedia.org/wiki/Sparse_matrix*), then we can use specific variants of joins to compute more efficiently in parallel. A join has a *lefthand side* (LHS) branch and one or more *righthand side* (RHS) branches. Cascading includes a HashJoin (*http://bit.ly/14NXTQA*) when the data for all but one branch is small enough to fit into memory. In other words, given some insights about the "shape" of the data, when we have a large data set (nonsparse) we can join with one or more small data sets (sparse) in memory. HashJoin implements a nonblocking "asymmetrical join" or "replicated join," where the leftmost side will not block (accumulate into memory) in order to complete the join, but the rightmost sides will. So we

put the sparser data on the righthand side to leverage the performance benefits of the
HashJoin.

Keep in mind that stop words lists tend to be bounded at approximately 10^5 keywords.
That is relatively sparse when compared with an arbitrarily large token stream. At typical
"web scale," text analytics use cases may be processing billions of tokens, i.e., several
orders of magnitude larger than our largest possible stop words list. Sounds like a great
use case for HashJoin.

Comparing with Apache Pig

When it comes to the subject of building workflows—specifically about other abstractions on top of Hadoop—perhaps the most frequent question about Cascading is how
it compares with Apache Hive and Apache Pig. Let's take a look at comparable implementations of the "Example 4: Replicated Joins" app in both Pig and Hive.

First you'll need to install Pig according to the documentation (*http://pig.apache.org/*),
in particular the "Getting Started" chapter. Unpack the download and set the PIG_HOME
and PIG_CLASSPATH environment variables. Be sure to include Pig in your PATH environment variable as well.

Starting from the source code directory that you cloned in Git, connect into the *part4*
subdirectory. The file *src/scripts/wc.pig* shows source for an Apache Pig (*http://
pig.apache.org/*) script that implements Word Count:

```
docPipe = LOAD '$docPath' USING PigStorage('\t', 'tagsource') AS (doc_id, text);
docPipe = FILTER docPipe BY doc_id != 'doc_id';

stopPipe = LOAD '$stopPath' USING PigStorage('\t', 'tagsource') AS (stop:chararray);
stopPipe = FILTER stopPipe BY stop != 'stop';

-- specify a regex operation to split the "document" text lines into a token stream
tokenPipe = FOREACH docPipe
  GENERATE doc_id, FLATTEN(TOKENIZE(LOWER(text), ' [](),.')) AS token;
tokenPipe = FILTER tokenPipe BY token MATCHES '\\w.*';

-- perform a left join to remove stop words, discarding the rows
-- which joined with stop words, i.e., were non-null after left join
tokenPipe = JOIN tokenPipe BY token LEFT, stopPipe BY stop;
tokenPipe = FILTER tokenPipe BY stopPipe::stop IS NULL;

-- determine the word counts
tokenGroups = GROUP tokenPipe BY token;
wcPipe = FOREACH tokenGroups
  GENERATE group AS token, COUNT(tokenPipe) AS count;

-- output
STORE wcPipe INTO '$wcPath' using PigStorage('\t', 'tagsource');
EXPLAIN -out dot/wc_pig.dot -dot wcPipe;
```

To run the Pig app:

```
$ rm -rf output
$ mkdir -p dot
$ pig -version
Warning: $HADOOP_HOME is deprecated.

Apache Pig version 0.10.0 (r1328203)
compiled Apr 19 2012, 22:54:12
$ pig -p docPath=./data/rain.txt -p wcPath=./output/wc -p \
    stopPath=./data/en.stop ./src/scripts/wc.pig
```

Output from this Pig script should be the same as the output from the Cascading sample app. To be fair, Pig has support for a replicated join, which is not shown here. We tried to get it working, but there were bugs.

Notice that the Pig source is reasonably similar to Cascading, and even a bit more compact. There are sources and sinks defined, tuple schemes, pipe assemblies, joins, functions, regex filters, aggregations, etc. Also, the EXPLAIN at the last line generates a flow diagram, which will be in the *dot/wc_pig.dot* file after the script runs.

Apache Pig is a data manipulation language (DML) (*http://bit.ly/12dSa3B*), which provides a query algebra atop Hadoop. It is easy to pick up and generally considered to have less of a learning curve when compared with Cascading—especially for people who are analysts, not J2EE developers. An interactive prompt called *Grunt* makes it simple to prototype apps. Also, Pig can be extended by writing user-defined functions in Java or other languages.

Some drawbacks may be encountered when using Pig for complex apps, particularly in Enterprise IT environments. Extensions via UDFs must be coded and built outside of the *Pig Latin* language. Similarly, integration of apps outside the context of Apache Hadoop generally requires other coding outside of the scripting language. Business logic must cross multiple language boundaries. This makes it increasingly difficult to troubleshoot code, optimize query plans, audit schema use, handle exceptions, set notifications, track data provenance, etc.

Also note that the LOAD and STORE statements use string literals to reference command-line arguments. These are analogous to taps in Cascading, except that in Pig the compiler won't be able to catch errors until runtime—which is problematic given that potentially expensive resources on the cluster are already being consumed. Using string literals for business logic tends to limit testability in general.

Another issue is much more nuanced: in Pig, the logical plan for a query is conflated with its physical plan. This implies a nondeterministic aspect to Pig's executions, because the number of maps and reduces may change unexpectedly as the data changes. This limits the ability to collect app history in "apples-to-apples" comparisons across different runs as your production data changes.

In short, simple problems are simple to do in Pig; hard problems become quite complex. For organizations that tend toward the "conservatism" end of a spectrum for programming environments, these issues with Pig increase risk at scale. Yahoo! has been able to scale out use of Apache Pig for a large organization; however, that will not typically be the case in many Enterprise verticals.

Comparing with Apache Hive

Now let's take a look at Apache Hive. You'll need to install Hive according to the documentation (*http://hive.apache.org/*) and in particular the "Getting Started" page in the wiki. Unpack the download, set the HIVE_HOME environment variable, and include the Hive binary in your PATH as well.

Starting from the source code directory that you cloned in Git, connect into the *part4* subdirectory. The file *src/scripts/wc.q* shows source for an Apache Hive (*http://hive.apache.org/*) script that approximates the Cascading code in "Example 4: Replicated Joins". To run this:

```
$ rm -rf derby.log metastore_db/
$ hive -hiveconf hive.metastore.warehouse.dir=/tmp < src/scripts/wc.q
```

The first line will clear out any metadata from a previous run. Otherwise the jobs would fail. For larger apps, Hive requires a metadata store in some relational database. However, the examples of Hive here could use an embedded metastore.

For the sake of space, we don't show all the output from Hive. An example is shown in the GitHub gist for "Example 4: Replicated Joins".

Looking at that Hive source code, first we prepare the data definition language (DDL) for loading the raw data:

```
CREATE TABLE raw_docs (doc_id STRING, text STRING)
ROW FORMAT DELIMITED
FIELDS TERMINATED BY '\t'
STORED AS TEXTFILE;

CREATE TABLE raw_stop (stop STRING)
ROW FORMAT DELIMITED
FIELDS TERMINATED BY '\t'
STORED AS TEXTFILE;

LOAD DATA
LOCAL INPATH 'data/rain.txt'
OVERWRITE INTO TABLE raw_docs;

LOAD DATA
LOCAL INPATH 'data/en.stop'
OVERWRITE INTO TABLE raw_stop;
```

Next, we strip off the headers from the TSV files (anybody know a better approach for this?):

```
CREATE TABLE docs (doc_id STRING, text STRING);

INSERT OVERWRITE TABLE docs
SELECT * FROM raw_docs WHERE doc_id <> 'doc_id';

CREATE TABLE stop (stop STRING);

INSERT OVERWRITE TABLE stop
SELECT * FROM raw_stop WHERE stop <> 'stop';
```

Then we tokenize using an external Python script, which also handles scrubbing the tokens:

```
CREATE TABLE tokens (token STRING);

INSERT OVERWRITE TABLE tokens
SELECT TRANSFORM(text) USING 'python ./src/scripts/tokenizer.py' AS token
FROM docs;
```

Let's take a look at that Python script, too—this is an alternative approach for creating UDFs:

```python
#!/usr/bin/env python
# encoding: utf-8

import re
import sys

pat_l = re.compile("\w.*")
pat_r = re.compile(".*\w")

def tokenize (line):
    """
    split a line of text into a stream of tokens,
    while scrubbing the tokens
    """
    for token in map(lambda t1: re.search(pat_r, t1).group(),
                     map(lambda t0: re.search(pat_l, t0).group(),
                         line.split(" "))):
        if len(token) > 0:
            yield token

if __name__ == "__main__":
    for line in sys.stdin:
        for token in tokenize(line.strip().lower()):
            print token
```

Finally, filter with a left join, then group and count:

```
SELECT token, COUNT(*) AS count
FROM (
```

```
SELECT
  *
FROM tokens LEFT OUTER JOIN stop
  ON (tokens.token = stop.stop)
  WHERE stop IS NULL
) t
GROUP BY token
;
```

The results should be the same as the output from "Example 4: Replicated Joins" in Cascading. As you can see from this example, the expression of the last query is relatively compact and easy to understand. Getting input data into Hive required a few backflips. We didn't show the part about getting data out, but it's essentially an HDFS file, and you'll need to manage your ETL process outside of Hive.

There are several advantages for using Hive:

- Hive is the most popular abstraction atop Apache Hadoop.
- Hive has a SQL-like language where the syntax is familiar for most analysts.
- Hive makes it simple to load large-scale unstructured data and run ad hoc queries.
- Hive provides many built-in functions for statistics, JSON, XPath, etc.

It is easy to understand on the surface, given that SQL is the lingua franca of Enterprise data. However, a typical concern voiced in Enterprise IT environments is that while Hive provides a SQL-like syntax, it is not compliant with the ANSI SQL (*http://bit.ly/14R3PYK*) spec. Hive's behaviors contradict what people expect from SQL and relational databases. For example, nondeterministic execution of queries—particularly when Hive attempts to use different join strategies—implies big surprises at scale during runtime.

Many years ago when Enterprise firms were considering SQL databases as new technology, the predictability of runtime costs was a factor driving adoption. Although the HQL of Hive is familiar as SQL, the predictability of runtime costs is not available.

Other issues found with Pig also apply to Hive:

- Integration generally requires code outside the scripting language.
- Business logic must cross multiple language boundaries.
- It becomes difficult to represent complex workflows, machine learning algorithms, etc.

Again, all of this makes Hive increasingly difficult to troubleshoot, optimize, audit, handle exceptions, set notifications, track data provenance, etc., for Enterprise data workflows. Each "bug" may require hours or even days before its context can be reproduced in a test environment. Complexity of the software grows, and so does the associated risk.

## CHAPTER 3

Test-Driven Development

Example 5: TF-IDF Implementation

In the previous example, we looked at extending pipe assemblies in Cascading workflows. Functionally, "Example 4: Replicated Joins" is only a few changes away from implementing an algorithm called term frequency–inverse document frequency (TF-IDF) (*http://en.wikipedia.org/wiki/Tf*idf*). This is the basis for many search indexing metrics, such as in the popular open source search engine Apache Lucene (*http://lucene.apache.org/*). See the Similarity class (*http://bit.ly/13skx44*) in Lucene for a great discussion of the algorithm and its use.

For this example, let's show how to implement TF-IDF in Cascading—which is a useful subassembly to reuse in a variety of apps. Figure 3-1 shows a conceptual diagram for this. Based on having a more complex app to work with, we'll begin to examine Cascading features for testing at scale.

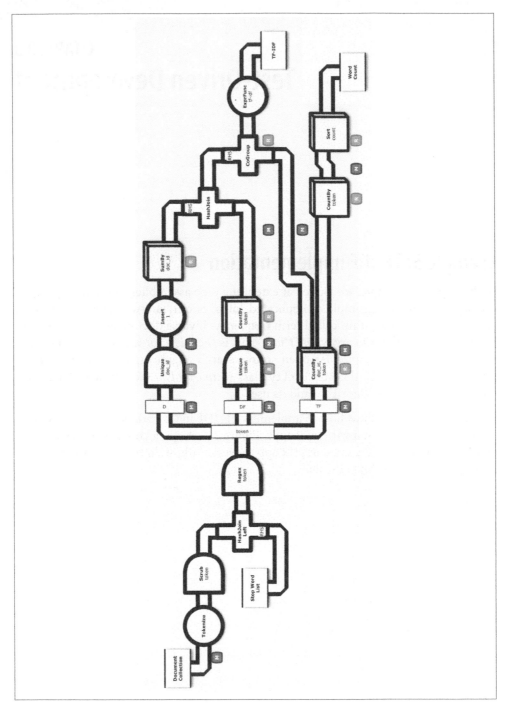

Figure 3-1. Conceptual flow diagram for "Example 5: TF-IDF Implementation"

Starting from the source code directory that you cloned in Git, connect into the *part5* subdirectory. First let's add another sink tap to write the TF-IDF weights:

```
String tfidfPath = args[ 3 ];
Tap tfidfTap = new Hfs( new TextDelimited( true, "\t" ), tfidfPath );
```

Next we'll modify the existing pipe assemblies for Word Count, beginning immediately after the join used as a "stop words" filter. We add the following line to retain only the doc_id and token fields in the output tuple stream, based on the fieldSelector parameter:

```
tokenPipe = new Retain( tokenPipe, fieldSelector );
```

Now let's step back and consider the desired end result, a TF-IDF metric. The "TF" and "IDF" parts of TF-IDF can be calculated given four metrics:

Term count
> Number of times a given token appears in a given document

Document frequency
> How frequently a given token appears across all documents

Number of terms
> Total number of tokens in a given document

Document count
> Total number of documents

Slight modifications to Word Count produce both term count and document frequency, along with the other two components, which get calculated almost as by-products.

At this point, we need to use the tuple stream in multiple ways—effectively splitting the intermediate results from tokenPipe in three ways. Note that there are three basic patterns for separating or combining tuple streams:

Merge
> Combine two or more streams that have identical fields

Join
> Combine two or more streams that have different fields, based on common field values

Split
> Take a single stream and send it down two or more pipes, each with unique branch names

We've already seen a join; now we'll introduce a split. This is also a good point to talk about the names of branches in pipe assemblies. Note that pipes always have names. When we connect pipes into pipe assemblies, the name gets inherited downstream—unless it gets changed through the API or due to a structural difference such as a join or a merge. Branch names are important for troubleshooting and instrumentation of workflows. In this case where we're using a split, Cascading requires each branch to have a different name.

The first branch after `tokenPipe` calculates *term counts*, as shown in Figure 3-2. We'll call that pipe assembly `tfPipe`, with a branch name TF:

```
// one branch of the flow tallies the token counts for term frequency (TF)
Pipe tfPipe = new Pipe( "TF", tokenPipe );
Fields tf_count = new Fields( "tf_count" );
tfPipe = new CountBy( tfPipe, new Fields( "doc_id", "token" ), tf_count );

Fields tf_token = new Fields( "tf_token" );
tfPipe = new Rename( tfPipe, token, tf_token );
```

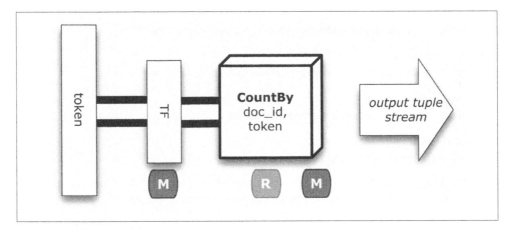

Figure 3-2. Term frequency branch

This uses a built-in *partial aggregate* operation called CountBy (*http://bit.ly/12GYNv4*), which counts duplicates in a tuple stream. Partial aggregates are quite useful for parallelizing algorithms efficiently. Portions of an aggregation—for example, a summation—can be performed in different tasks.

We also rename `token` to `tf_token` so that it won't conflict with other tuple streams in a subsequent join. At this point, we have the term counts.

The next branch may seem less than intuitive...and it is a bit odd, but efficient. We need to calculate the *total number of documents*, in a way that can be consumed later in a join. So we'll produce total document count as a field, in each tuple for the RHS of the join. That keeps our workflow parallel, allowing the calculations to scale out horizontally. We'll call that pipe assembly `dPipe`, with a branch name D, as shown in Figure 3-3. Alternatively, we could calculate the total number of documents outside of this workflow and pass it along as a parameter, or use a distributed counter.

```
Fields doc_id = new Fields( "doc_id" );
Fields tally = new Fields( "tally" );
Fields rhs_join = new Fields( "rhs_join" );
Fields n_docs = new Fields( "n_docs" );
Pipe dPipe = new Unique( "D", tokenPipe, doc_id );
dPipe = new Each( dPipe, new Insert( tally, 1 ), Fields.ALL );
dPipe = new Each( dPipe, new Insert( rhs_join, 1 ), Fields.ALL );
dPipe = new SumBy( dPipe, rhs_join, tally, n_docs, long.class );
```

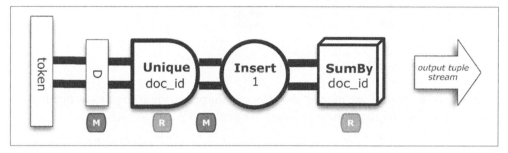

Figure 3-3. Document counts branch

This filters for the unique doc_id values and then uses another built-in partial aggregate
operation called SumBy (*http://bit.ly/10zJwjj*), which sums values associated with duplicate keys in a tuple stream. Great, now we've got the document count. Notice that the
results are named rhs_join, preparing for the subsequent join.

The third branch calculates *document frequency* for each token. We'll call that pipe
assembly dfPipe, with a branch name DF, as shown in Figure 3-4:

```
// one branch tallies the token counts for document frequency (DF)

Pipe dfPipe = new Unique( "DF", tokenPipe, Fields.ALL );
Fields df_count = new Fields( "df_count" );
dfPipe = new CountBy( dfPipe, token, df_count );

Fields df_token = new Fields( "df_token" );
Fields lhs_join = new Fields( "lhs_join" );
dfPipe = new Rename( dfPipe, token, df_token );
dfPipe = new Each( dfPipe, new Insert( lhs_join, 1 ), Fields.ALL );
```

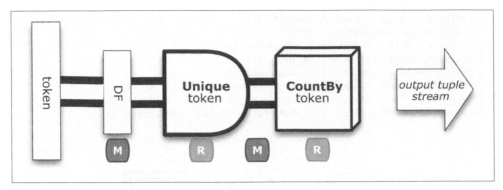

Figure 3-4. Document frequency branch

Notice that the results are named `lhs_join`, again preparing for the subsequent join. Now we have all the components needed to calculate TF-IDF weights.

To finish the calculations in parallel, we'll use two different kinds of joins in Cascading —a HashJoin (*http://bit.ly/14NXTQA*) followed by a CoGroup (*http://bit.ly/1aCSulv*). Figure 3-5 shows how these joins merge the three branches together:

```
// join to bring together all the components for calculating TF-IDF
// the D side of the join is smaller, so it goes on the RHS
Pipe idfPipe = new HashJoin( dfPipe, lhs_join, dPipe, rhs_join );

// the IDF side of the join is smaller, so it goes on the RHS
Pipe tfidfPipe = new CoGroup( tfPipe, tf_token, idfPipe, df_token );
```

We used `HashJoin` previously for a replicated join. In this case we know that document count will not be a large amount of data, so it works for the RHS. The other join, `CoGroup`, handles a more general case where the RHS cannot be kept entirely in memory. In those cases a threshold can be adjusted for "spill," where RHS tuples get moved to disk.

Then we calculate TF-IDF weights using an ExpressionFunction (*http://bit.ly/10zJCYg*) in Cascading:

```
// calculate the TF-IDF weights, per token, per document
Fields tfidf = new Fields( "tfidf" );
String expression =
  "(double) tf_count * Math.log( (double) n_docs / ( 1.0 + df_count ) )";
ExpressionFunction tfidfExpression =
  new ExpressionFunction( tfidf, expression, Double.class );
Fields tfidfArguments = new Fields( "tf_count", "df_count", "n_docs" );
tfidfPipe =
  new Each( tfidfPipe, tfidfArguments, tfidfExpression, Fields.ALL );

fieldSelector = new Fields( "tf_token", "doc_id", "tfidf" );
tfidfPipe = new Retain( tfidfPipe, fieldSelector );
tfidfPipe = new Rename( tfidfPipe, tf_token, token );
```

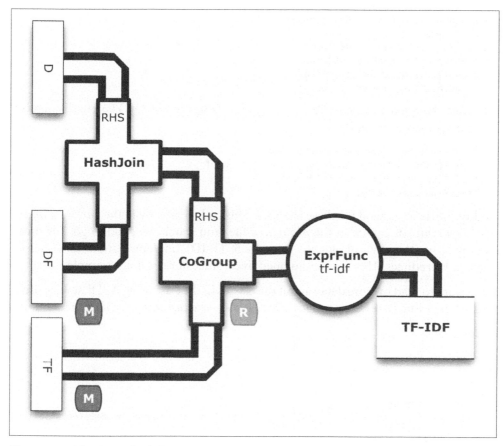

Figure 3-5. TF-IDF calculation

Now we can get back to the rest of the workflow. Let's keep the Word Count metrics, because those become useful when testing. This branch uses CountBy as well, to optimize better than "Example 4: Replicated Joins":

```
// keep track of the word counts, which are useful for QA
Pipe wcPipe = new Pipe( "wc", tfPipe );

Fields count = new Fields( "count" );
wcPipe = new SumBy( wcPipe, tf_token, tf_count, count, long.class );
wcPipe = new Rename( wcPipe, tf_token, token );

// additionally, sort by count
wcPipe = new GroupBy( wcPipe, count, count );
```

Last, we'll add another sink tap to the FlowDef (*http://bit.ly/11gRYXk*), for the TF-IDF output data:

```
// connect the taps, pipes, etc., into a flow
FlowDef flowDef = FlowDef.flowDef()
 .setName( "tfidf" )
 .addSource( docPipe, docTap )
 .addSource( stopPipe, stopTap )
 .addTailSink( tfidfPipe, tfidfTap )
 .addTailSink( wcPipe, wcTap );
```

We'll also change the name of the resulting Flow (*http://bit.ly/15gfV06*), to distinguish this from previous examples:

```
// write a DOT file and run the flow
Flow tfidfFlow = flowConnector.connect( flowDef );
tfidfFlow.writeDOT( "dot/tfidf.dot" );
tfidfFlow.complete();
```

Modify the `Main` method for these changes. This code is already in the *part5/src/main/ java/impatient/* directory, in the *Main.java* file. You should be good to go. For those keeping score, the physical plan in "Example 5: TF-IDF Implementation" now uses 11 maps and 9 reduces. That amount jumped by 5x since our previous example.

If you want to read in more detail about the classes in the Cascading API that were used, see the Cascading *User Guide* and *JavaDoc* (*http://www.cascading.org/documentation/*).

To build:

```
$ gradle clean jar
```

To run:

```
$ rm -rf output
$ hadoop jar ./build/libs/impatient.jar data/rain.txt output/wc data/en.stop \
    output/tfidf
```

Output text gets stored in the partition file *output/tfidf*, and you can verify the first 10 lines (including the header) by using the following:

```
$ head output/tfidf/part-00000
doc_id  tfidf                 token
doc02   0.9162907318741551    air
doc01   0.44628710262841953   area
doc03   0.22314355131420976   area
doc02   0.22314355131420976   area
doc05   0.9162907318741551    australia
doc05   0.9162907318741551    broken
doc04   0.9162907318741551    california's
doc04   0.9162907318741551    cause
doc02   0.9162907318741551    cloudcover
```

A gist on GitHub (*https://gist.github.com/3043791*) shows building and running "Example 5: TF-IDF Implementation". If your run looks terribly different, something is probably not set up correctly. Ask the developer community for troubleshooting advice.

By the way, did you notice what the TF-IDF weights for the tokens rain and shadow were? Those represent what these documents all have in common. How do those compare with weights for the other tokens? Conversely, consider the weight for australia (high weight) or area (different weights).

TF-IDF calculates a metric for each token, which indicates how "important" that token is to a document within the context of a collection of documents. The metric is calculated based on relative frequencies. On one hand, tokens that appear in most documents tend to have very low TF-IDF weights. On the other hand, tokens that are less common but appear multiple times in a few documents tend to have very high TF-IDF weights.

Note that information retrieval papers use token and term almost interchangeably in some cases. More advanced text analytics might calculate metrics for phrases, in which case a term becomes a more complex structure. However, we're only looking at single words.

Example 6: TF-IDF with Testing

Now that we have a more complex workflow for TF-IDF, let's consider best practices for test-driven development (TDD) (*http://bit.ly/10YXfTw*) at scale. We'll add unit tests into the build, then show how to leverage TDD features that are unique to Cascading: checkpoints, traps, assertions, etc. Figure 3-6 shows a conceptual diagram for this app.

Generally speaking, TDD starts off with a failing test, and then you code until the test passes. We'll start with a working app, with tests that pass—followed by discussion of how to use assertions for the test/code cycle.

Starting from the source code directory that you cloned in Git, connect into the *part6* subdirectory. As a first step toward better testing, let's add a unit test and show how it fits into this example. We need to add support for testing into our build. In the Gradle (*http://www.gradle.org/*) build script *build.gradle* we need to modify the compile task to include JUnit (*http://www.junit.org/*) and other testing dependencies:

```
dependencies {
  compile( 'cascading:cascading-core:2.1.+' ) { exclude group: 'log4j' }
  compile( 'cascading:cascading-hadoop:2.1.+' ) { transitive = true }

  testCompile( 'cascading:cascading-test:2.1.+' )
  testCompile( 'org.apache.hadoop:hadoop-test:1.0.+' )
  testCompile( 'junit:junit:4.8.+' )
}
```

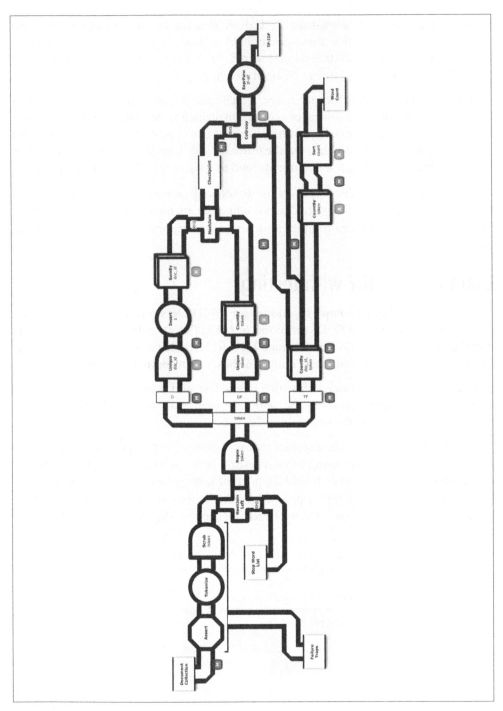

Figure 3-6. Conceptual flow diagram for "Example 6: TF-IDF with Testing"

Then we'll add a new `test` task to the build:

```
test {
  include 'impatient/**'

  //makes standard streams (err, out) visible at console when running tests
  testLogging.showStandardStreams = true

  //listening to test execution events
  beforeTest { descriptor ->
    logger.lifecycle("Running test: " + descriptor)
  }
  onOutput { descriptor, event ->
    logger.lifecycle("Test: " + descriptor + " produced standard out/err: "
      + event.message )
  }
}
```

A little restructuring of the source directories is required—see this GitHub code repo (*https://github.com/Cascading/Impatient/tree/master/part6*) where that is already set up properly.

The custom function `ScrubFunction` used to scrub tokens in "Example 3: Customized Operations" on page 17 had an additional method, to make unit testing simpler. We add a unit test in a new class called `ScrubTest.java`, which extends CascadingTestCase (*http://bit.ly/12GZ9Sh*):

```
public class ScrubTest extends CascadingTestCase
  {
  @Test
  public void testScrub()
    {
    Fields fieldDeclaration = new Fields( "doc_id", "token" );
    Function scrub = new ScrubFunction( fieldDeclaration );
    Tuple[] arguments = new Tuple[]{
      new Tuple( "doc_1", "FoO" ),
      new Tuple( "doc_1", " BAR " ),
      new Tuple( "doc_1", "     " ) // will be scrubbed
    };

    ArrayList<Tuple> expectResults = new ArrayList<Tuple>();
    expectResults.add( new Tuple( "doc_1", "foo" ) );
    expectResults.add( new Tuple( "doc_1", "bar" ) );

    TupleListCollector collector =
      invokeFunction( scrub, arguments, Fields.ALL );

    Iterator<Tuple> it = collector.iterator();
    ArrayList<Tuple> results = new ArrayList<Tuple>();

    while( it.hasNext() )
      results.add( it.next() );
```

```
        assertEquals( "Scrubbed result is not expected", expectResults, results );
      }
    }
```

Again, this is a particularly good place for a unit test. Scrubbing tokens is a likely point where edge cases will get encountered at scale. In practice, you'd want to define even more unit tests.

Going back to the *Main.java* module, let's see how to handle other kinds of unexpected issues with data at scale. We'll add both a *trap* and a *checkpoint* as taps:

```
    String trapPath = args[ 4 ];
    String checkPath = args[ 5 ];
    Tap trapTap = new Hfs( new TextDelimited( true, "\t" ), trapPath );
    Tap checkTap = new Hfs( new TextDelimited( true, "\t" ), checkPath );
```

Next we'll modify the head of the pipe assembly for documents to incorporate a *stream assertion*, as Figure 3-7 shows. This uses an AssertMatches (*http://bit.ly/11h1d9U*) to define the expected pattern for data in the input tuple stream. There could be quite a large number of documents, so it stands to reason that some data may become corrupted. In our case, another line has been added to the example input *data/rain.txt* to exercise the assertion and trap.

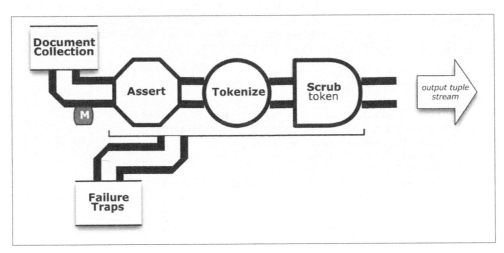

Figure 3-7. Stream assertion and failure trap

Notice in Figure 3-7 how the trap will apply to the entire branch that includes the stream assertion. Then we apply AssertionLevel.STRICT (*http://bit.ly/18w6RHF*) to force validation of the data:

```
// use a stream assertion to validate the input data
Pipe docPipe = new Pipe( "token" );
AssertMatches assertMatches = new AssertMatches( "doc\\d+\\s.*" );
docPipe = new Each( docPipe, AssertionLevel.STRICT, assertMatches );
```

Sometimes, when working with complex workflows, we just need to see what the tuple stream looks like. To show this feature, we'll insert a Debug (*http://bit.ly/14R4Ccc*) operation on the *DF* branch and use DebugLevel.VERBOSE (*http://bit.ly/13slgSV*) to trace the tuple values in the flow there:

```
// example use of a debug, to observe tuple stream; turn off below
dfPipe = new Each( dfPipe, DebugLevel.VERBOSE, new Debug( true ) );
```

This prints the tuple values at that point to the log file. Fortunately, it can be disabled with a single line—in practice, you'd probably use a command-line argument to control that.

Next let's show how to use a Checkpoint (*http://bit.ly/16OMCkh*) that forces the tuple stream to be persisted to HDFS. Figure 3-8 shows this inserted after the join of the *DF* and *D* branches.

```
// create a checkpoint, to observe the intermediate data in DF stream
Checkpoint idfCheck = new Checkpoint( "checkpoint", idfPipe );
Pipe tfidfPipe = new CoGroup( tfPipe, tf_token, idfCheck, df_token );
```

Checkpoints help especially when there is an expensive unit of work—such as a lengthy calculation. On one hand, if a calculation fits into a single map and several branches consume from it, then a checkpoint avoids having to redo the calculation for each branch. On the other hand, if a Hadoop job step fails, for whatever reason, then the Cascading app can be restarted from the last successful checkpoint.

At this point we have a relatively more complex set of taps to connect in the FlowDef (*http://bit.ly/11gRYXk*), to include the new output data for test-related features:

```
// connect the taps, pipes, traps, checkpoints, etc., into a flow
FlowDef flowDef = FlowDef.flowDef()
 .setName( "tfidf" )
 .addSource( docPipe, docTap )
 .addSource( stopPipe, stopTap )
 .addTailSink( tfidfPipe, tfidfTap )
 .addTailSink( wcPipe, wcTap )
 .addTrap( docPipe, trapTap )
 .addCheckpoint( idfCheck, checkTap );
```

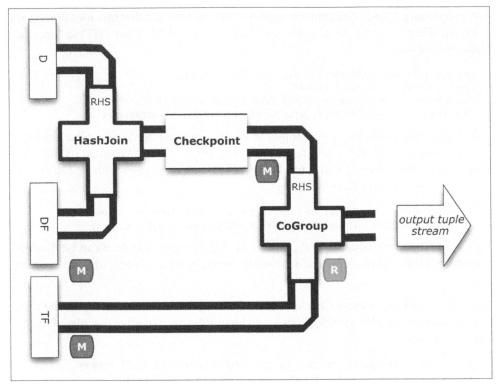

Figure 3-8. Checkpoint

Last, we'll specify the *verbosity* level for the debug trace and the *strictness* level for the stream assertion:

```
// set to DebugLevel.VERBOSE for trace,
// or DebugLevel.NONE in production
flowDef.setDebugLevel( DebugLevel.VERBOSE );

// set to AssertionLevel.STRICT for all assertions,
// or AssertionLevel.NONE in production
flowDef.setAssertionLevel( AssertionLevel.STRICT );
```

Modify the `Main` method for those changes. This code is already in the *part6/src/main/java/impatient/* directory, in the *Main.java* file. You should be good to go.

For those keeping score, the physical plan for "Example 6: TF-IDF with Testing" now uses 12 maps and 9 reduces. In other words, we added one map as the overhead for gaining lots of test features.

To build:

```
$ gradle clean jar
```

To run:

```
$ rm -rf output
$ hadoop jar ./build/libs/impatient.jar data/rain.txt output/wc data/en.stop \
    output/tfidf output/trap output/check
```

Remember that *data/rain.txt* has another row, intended to cause a trap. The output log should include a warning based on the stream assertion, which looks like this:

```
12/08/06 14:15:07 WARN stream.TrapHandler: exception trap on branch: 'token',
  for fields: [{2}:'doc_id', 'text'] tuple: ['zoink', 'null']
cascading.operation.AssertionException: argument tuple:
  ['zoink', 'null'] did not match: doc\d+\s.*
    at cascading.operation.assertion.BaseAssertion.throwFail(BaseAssertion.java:107)
    at cascading.operation.assertion.AssertMatches.doAssert(AssertMatches.java:84)
```

That is expected behavior. We asked Cascading to show warnings when stream assertions failed. The data that caused this warning gets trapped.

Not too far after that point in the log, there should be some other debug output that looks like the following:

```
12/08/06 14:15:46 INFO hadoop.FlowReducer: sinking to:
TempHfs["SequenceFile[ ['df_count', 'df_token', 'lhs_join']]"][DF/93669/]
['df_count', 'df_token', 'lhs_join']
['1', 'air', '1']
['3', 'area', '1']
['1', 'australia', '1']
['1', 'broken', '1']
```

Plus several more similar lines. That is the result of our debug trace.

Output text gets stored in the partition file *output/tfidf* as before. We also have the checkpointed data now:

```
$ head output/check/part-00000
```

df_count	df_token	lhs_join	rhs_join	n_docs
1	air	1	1	5
3	area	1	1	5
1	australia	1	1	5
1	broken	1	1	5
1	california's	1	1	5
1	cause	1	1	5
1	cloudcover	1	1	5
1	death	1	1	5
1	deserts	1	1	5

Also notice the data tuple trapped in `output/trap`:

```
$ cat output/trap/part-m-00001-00000

zoink null
```

That tuple does not match the regex doc\\d+\\s.* that was specified by the stream assertion. Great, we caught it before it blew up something downstream.

A gist on GitHub (*https://gist.github.com/3044049*) shows building and running "Example 6: TF-IDF with Testing". If your run looks terribly different, something is probably not set up correctly. Ask the developer community for troubleshooting advice.

A Word or Two About Testing

At first glance, the notion of TDD (*http://bit.ly/10YXfTw*) might seem a bit antithetical in the context of Big Data. After all, TDD is supposed to be about short development cycles, writing automated test cases that are intended to fail, and lots of refactoring. Those descriptions don't seem to fit with batch jobs that involve terabytes of data run on huge Hadoop clusters for days before they complete.

Stated in a somewhat different way, according to Kent Beck, TDD "encourages simple designs and inspires confidence." That statement fits quite well with the philosophy of Cascading. The Cascading API is intended to provide a pattern language for working with large-scale data—GroupBy, Join, Count, Regex, Filter—so that the need for writing custom functions becomes relatively rare. That speaks to "encouraging simple designs" directly. The practice in Cascading of modeling business process and orchestrating Apache Hadoop workflows speaks to "inspiring confidence" in a big way.

So now we'll let the cat out of the bag for a little secret…working with unstructured data at scale has been shown to be quite valuable by the likes of Google, Amazon, eBay, Facebook, LinkedIn, Twitter, etc. However, most of the "heavy lifting" that we perform in MapReduce workflows is essentially cleaning up data. DJ Patil, formerly Chief Scientist at LinkedIn, explains this point quite eloquently in the mini-book *Data Jujitsu* (*http://radar.oreilly.com/2012/07/data-jujitsu.html*):

> It's impossible to overstress this: 80% of the work in any data project is in cleaning the data… Work done up front in getting clean data will be amply repaid over the course of the project.
>
> — DJ Patil
> *Data Jujitsu (2012)*

Cleaning up unstructured data allows for subsequent use of sampling techniques (*http://en.wikipedia.org/wiki/Sampling*), dimensional reduction (*http://en.wikipedia.org/wiki/Dimension_reduction*), and other practices that help alleviate some of the bottlenecks that might otherwise be encountered in Enterprise data workflows. Thinking about this in another way, we have need for API features that demonstrate how "dirty" data has been cleaned up. Cascading provides those features, which turn out to be quite valuable in practice.

Common practices for test-driven development include writing unit tests (*http://en.wikipedia.org/wiki/Unit_test*) or mocks (*http://en.wikipedia.org/wiki/Mock_object*). How does one write a quick unit test for a Godzilla-sized data set?

The short answer is: you don't. However, you can greatly reduce the need for writing unit test coverage by limiting the amount of custom code required. Hopefully we've shown that aspect of Cascading by now. Beyond that, you can use sampling techniques to quantify confidence that an app has run correctly. You can also define system tests at scale in relatively simple ways. Furthermore, you can define contingencies for what to do when assumptions fail…as they inevitably do, at scale.

Let's discuss sampling. Generally speaking, large MapReduce workflows tend to be relatively opaque processes that are difficult to observe. Cascading, however, provides two techniques for observing portions of a workflow. One very simple approach is to insert a Debug (*http://bit.ly/14R4Ccc*) into a pipe to see the tuple values passing through a particular part of a workflow. Debug output goes to the log instead of a file, but it can be turned off, e.g., with a command-line option. If the data is large, one can use a Sample (*http://bit.ly/12G7z0N*) filter to sample the tuple values that get written to the log.

Another approach is to use a Checkpoint (*http://bit.ly/16OMCkh*), which forces intermediate data to be written out to HDFS. This may also become important for performance reasons, i.e., forcing results to disk to avoid recomputing—e.g., when there are multiple uses for the output of a pipe downstream such as with the RHS of a HashJoin (*http://bit.ly/14NXTQA*). Sampling may be performed either before (with Debug) or after (with Checkpoint) the data gets persisted to HDFS. Checkpoints can also be used to restart partially failed workflows, to recover some costs.

Next, let's talk about system tests. Cascading includes support for stream assertions (*http://bit.ly/10zK4FV*). These provide mechanisms for asserting that the values in a tuple stream meet certain criteria—similar to the `assert` keyword in Java, or an `assert not null` in a JUnit test. We can assert patterns *strictly* as unit tests during development and then run testing against regression data. For performance reasons, we might use command-line options to turn off assertions in production—or keep them (fail-fast mode) if a use case requires that level of guarantee.

Books about Test Driven Development

For more information about TDD in general, check out these books:

- *Test Driven Development: By Example* by Kent Beck (Addison-Wesley)
- *Test-Driven Development: A Practical Guide* by Dave Astels (Prentice Hall)

Lastly, what should you do when assumptions fail? One lesson of working with data at scale is that the best assumptions will inevitably fail. Unexpected things happen, and 80% of the work will be cleaning up problems.

Cascading defines failure traps (*http://bit.ly/19YhYKB*), which capture data that would otherwise cause an operation to fail, e.g., by throwing an exception. For example, perhaps 99% of the cases in your log files can be rolled up into a set of standard reports… but 1% requires manual review. Great, process the 99% that work and shunt the 1% failure cases into a special file marked "For manual review." That can be turned into a report for the customer support department. Keep in mind, however, that traps are intended for handling exceptional cases. If you know in advance how to categorize good versus bad data, then a best practice is to use a filter instead of a trap (*http://bit.ly/17TNgBR*).

## CHAPTER 4

Scalding—A Scala DSL for Cascading

Why Use Scalding?

Cascading represents a pattern language where we use a "plumbing" metaphor with pipes and operators to build workflows. Looking at sample code in the previous chapter, the Java source requires much more detail than simply pipes and operators. Even so, we can use conceptual flow diagrams to keep track of the plumbing—the actual logic of what is being performed by a workflow. What if we could simply write code at the level of detail in those diagrams?

Scalding is a domain-specific language (DSL) (*http://www.scala-lang.org/node/1403*) in the Scala programming language, which integrates Cascading. The functional programming paradigm used in Scala is much closer than Java to the original model for MapReduce. Consequently, Scalding source code for workflows has a nearly 1:1 correspondence with the concise visual descriptions in our conceptual flow diagrams. In other words, developers work directly in the plumbing of pipes, where the pattern language becomes immediately visible. That aspect alone brings incredible advantages for software engineering with very large-scale data. Apps written in Java with the Cascading API almost seem like assembly language programming in comparison. Plus, Scala offers other advanced programming models used in large-scale Enterprise work such as the actor model (*http://www.scala-lang.org/node/242*) for concurrency.

While Scalding builds on Cascading, other libraries build atop Scalding—including support for type-safe libraries, abstract algebra, very large sparse matrices, etc., which are used to implement distributed algorithms and robust infrastructure for data services. For example, simple operations such as calculating a running median can become hard problems when you are servicing hundreds of millions of customers with tight requirements for service-level agreements (SLAs). A running median is an example of a metric needed in anti-fraud classifiers, social recommenders, customer segmentation, etc. Scalding offers simple, concise ways to implement distributed algorithms for that kind of analysis. Those aspects are particularly important for the scale of operations at firms such as Twitter, eBay, LinkedIn, Etsy, etc., where Scalding is deployed.

Keep in mind that Apache Hadoop is based on the MapReduce research made public by Google nearly a decade ago. MapReduce became an important component of Google's internal technology for large-scale batch workflows. Meanwhile, Google has continued to evolve its infrastructure; estimates place its current technology stack at least three generations beyond the original MapReduce work. The public sees only portions of that massive R&D effort (e.g., in papers about Dremel (*http://bit.ly/14qTgNn*), Pregel (*http://bit.ly/14qThku*), etc.).

What becomes clear from the published works is that Google scientists and engineers leverage advanced techniques based on abstract algebra, linear algebra for very large sparse matrices, sketches, etc., to build robust, efficient infrastructure at massive scale. Scalding represents a relatively public view of comparable infrastructure.

Let's start here with a few simple examples in Scalding. Given a few subtle changes in the code, some of our brief examples can be turned into state-of-the-art parallel processing at scale. For instance, check out the PageRank implementation shown in the Scalding source, and also these sample recommender systems written by Twitter (*http://engineering.twitter.com/2012/03/generating-recommendations-with.html*).

Getting Started with Scalding

The best resource for getting started with Scalding is the project wiki page on GitHub (*https://github.com/twitter/scalding/wiki/Getting-Started*).

In addition to Git and Java, which were set up in Chapter 1, you will need to have a few other platforms and tools installed for the examples in this chapter:

Scala (http://www.scala-lang.org/downloads)
   Current version of Scalding works with Scala versions 2.8.1, 2.9.1, 2.9.2.

Simple Build Tool, a.k.a. SBT (http://bit.ly/1aCU330)
   Must be version 0.11.3.

Ruby (http://www.ruby-lang.org/)
   Required for the *scald.rb* script; most recent stable release.

Also, be sure to put the executable for sbt in your PATH.

The *scald.rb* script provides a limited command-line interface (CLI) for Scalding, so that one can conveniently compile and launch apps. Keep in mind that this is not a build system. For any serious work, you are better off using a build tool such as Gradle to create a "fat jar" that includes all the class dependencies that are not available on your Hadoop cluster. More about that later.

Connect somewhere you have space for downloads, and then use Git to clone the latest update from the master branch of the Scalding project on GitHub:

```
$ git clone git://github.com/twitter/scalding.git
```

Connect into that newly cloned directory and run the following steps with sbt to get Scalding set up:

```
$ cd scalding
$ export SCALDING_HOME=`pwd`
$ sbt update
$ sbt test
$ sbt assembly
```

These commands may take a few minutes to complete. Afterward, be sure to add the Scalding utility script in *scripts/scald.rb* to your path:

```
export PATH=`pwd`/scripts:$PATH
```

At this point, let's test to see if Scalding is set up properly. The *tutorial* directory includes code samples, and *Tutorial1.scala* provides a simplest possible app in Scalding:

```
import com.twitter.scalding._

class Tutorial1(args : Args) extends Job(args) {
  val input = TextLine("tutorial/data/hello.txt")
  val output = TextLine("tutorial/data/output1.txt")

  input
    .read
    .project('line)
    .write(output)
}
```

This is comparable with "Example 1: Simplest Possible App in Cascading" because it copies text lines from one file to another. The example uses text in the *tutorial/data/hello.txt* sample data file:

```
$ cat tutorial/data/hello.txt
Hello world
Goodbye world
```

To run this Scalding code:

```
$ scald.rb --local tutorial/Tutorial1.scala
12/12/25 09:58:16 INFO property.AppProps: using app.id: \
8A7F63D2D42594F9A1CD9B5DE08100E8
12/12/25 09:58:16 INFO util.Version: Concurrent, Inc - Cascading 2.0.2
12/12/25 09:58:16 INFO flow.Flow: [Tutorial1] starting
12/12/25 09:58:16 INFO flow.Flow: [Tutorial1]
  source: FileTap["TextLine[['num', 'line']->[ALL]]"]["tutorial/data/hello.txt"]"]
12/12/25 09:58:16 INFO flow.Flow: [Tutorial1]
  sink: FileTap["TextLine[['num', 'line']->[ALL]]"]["tutorial/data/output1.txt"]"]
12/12/25 09:58:16 INFO flow.Flow: [Tutorial1]  parallel execution is enabled: true
```

```
12/12/25 09:58:16 INFO flow.Flow: [Tutorial1]  starting jobs: 1
12/12/25 09:58:16 INFO flow.Flow: [Tutorial1]  allocating threads: 1
12/12/25 09:58:16 INFO flow.FlowStep: [Tutorial1] starting step: local
```

Then to confirm the results after the Scalding code has run:

```
$ cat tutorial/data/output1.txt
Hello world
Goodbye world
```

If your results look similar, you should be good to go.

Otherwise, if you have any troubles, contact the cascading-user email forum (*http://bit.ly/19U7Lvl*) or tweet to @Scalding on Twitter. Very helpful developers are available to assist.

Example 3 in Scalding: Word Count with Customized Operations

First, let's try a simple app in Scalding. Starting from the "Impatient" source code directory that you cloned in Git, connect into the *part8* subdirectory. Then we'll write a Word Count app in Scalding that includes a token scrub operation, similar to "Example 3: Customized Operations" on page 17:

```
import com.twitter.scalding._

class Example3(args : Args) extends Job(args) {
  Tsv(args("doc"), ('doc_id, 'text), skipHeader = true)
    .read
    .flatMap('text -> 'token) { text : String => text.split("[ \\[\\]\\(\\),.]") }
    .mapTo('token -> 'token) { token : String => scrub(token) }
    .filter('token) { token : String => token.length > 0 }
    .groupBy('token) { _.size('count) }
    .write(Tsv(args("wc"), writeHeader = true))

  def scrub(token : String) : String = {
    token
      .trim
      .toLowerCase
  }

  override def config(implicit mode: Mode): Map[AnyRef, AnyRef] = {
    // resolves "ClassNotFoundException cascading.*" exception on a cluster
    super.config(mode) ++ Map("cascading.app.appjar.class" -> classOf[Example3])
  }
}
```

Let's compare this code for Word Count with the conceptual flow diagram for "Example 3: Customized Operations", which is shown in Figure 4-1. The lines of Scalding source code have an almost 1:1 correspondence with the elements in this flow diagram. In other words, Scalding provides an almost pure expression of the DAG for this Cascading flow. This point underscores the expressiveness of the functional programming paradigm.

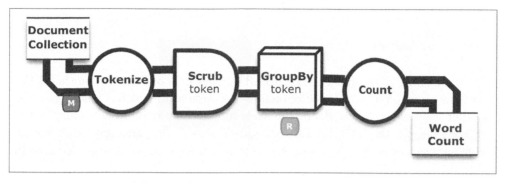

Figure 4-1. Conceptual flow diagram for "Example 3: Customized Operations"

Examining this app line by line, the first thing to note is that we extend the Job() base class in Scalding:

```
class Example3(args : Args) extends Job(args) { ... }
```

Next, the source tap reads tuples from a data set in TSV format. This expects to have a header, then doc_id and text as the fields. The tap identifier for the data set gets specified by a --doc command-line parameter:

```
Tsv(args("doc"), ('doc_id, 'text), skipHeader = true)
  .read
```

The flatMap() function in Scalding is equivalent to a generator in Cascading. It maps each element to a list, then flattens that list—emitting a Cascading result tuple for each item in the returned list. In this case, it splits text into tokens based on RegexSplitGen erator:

```
.flatMap('text -> 'token) { text : String => text.split("[ \\[\\]\\(\\),.]") }
```

In essence, Scalding extends the collections API in Scala. Scala has functional constructs such as *map, reduce, filter*, etc., built into the language, so the Cascading operations have been integrated as operations on its parallel iterators (*http://bit.ly/14qTpQW*). In other words, the notion of a *pipe* in Scalding is the same as a distributed list. That provides a powerful abstraction for large-scale parallel processing. Keep that in mind for later.

The mapTo() function in the next line shows how to call a customized function for scrubbing tokens. This is substantially simpler to do in Scalding:

```
.mapTo('token -> 'token) { token : String => scrub(token) }
.filter('token) { token : String => token.length > 0 }
```

Example 3 in Scalding: Word Count with Customized Operations | 55

Defining new functions in Scalding is also much simpler, as the following code snippet shows:

```
def scrub(token : String) : String = {
  token
    .trim
    .toLowerCase
}
```

A few dozen lines of Java have been replaced by a few lines of Scala. On one hand, that represents an order of magnitude reduction in source code, which is a huge gain. On the other hand, using Java to define this same function allows for finer-grained behaviors. For example, the `filter()` call was added to create the same semantics that the `ScrubFunction` implemented—whereas in Java that logic could be specified directly within the `operate()` method.

Java, as an object-oriented language, is arguably quite good for defining the low-level behaviors of Scala, as a functional programming language. Think of the Java code in Cascading as a kind of "assembly language" for Scalding. Moreover, there is an enormous number of available packages in Java that can be used by Scala. In fact, part of the reason for the *scald.rb* utility script is to integrate other Java packages into Scalding.

The next line performs the equivalent of a `GroupBy` aggregation in Cascading, followed by an `Every` and a `Count` operation. The `size()` function in Scala performs the token count:

```
.groupBy('token) { _.size('count) }
```

Finally, the sink tap writes tuples in the output stream to a data set in TSV format, including a header. The tap identifier for the output data set is defined by a `--wc` command-line parameter:

```
.write(Tsv(args("wc"), writeHeader = true))
```

Also note the configuration override:

```
override def config(implicit mode: Mode): Map[AnyRef, AnyRef] = { .. }
```

This resolves a `ClassNotFoundException` exception when running Scalding apps as fat jars on a remote Hadoop cluster. As of this writing (2013Q1) Twitter uses `sbt` to build Scalding apps for lots of deployments. However, other organizations have begun to use Maven, Gradle, etc., and for some reason apps created with these other build systems sometimes see exceptions when running fat jars on remote clusters. This workaround was created by Chris Severs at eBay to resolve the issue. Include it in each Scala class that defines a Scalding workflow.

This code is already in the *part8/src/main/scala/* directory, in the *Example3.scala* file. To build and run:

```
$ rm -rf output
$ scald.rb --hdfs-local src/main/scala/Example3.scala \
    --doc data/rain.txt --wc output/wc
```

In the output, the first 10 lines (including the header) should look like this:

```
$ head output/wc/part-00000
token        count
a            8
air          1
an           1
and          2
area         4
as           2
australia    1
back         1
broken       1
```

A gist on GitHub (*https://gist.github.com/4371896*) shows building and running this app. If your run looks terribly different, something is probably not set up correctly. Ask the developer community for troubleshooting advice.

A Word or Two about Functional Programming

At the mention of *functional programming*, Java is not quite the first programming language that comes to mind. Cascading, however, with its pattern language and plumbing metaphor, borrows much from the functional programming paradigm. For example, there is no concept of "mutable variables" in the context of a flow—just the stream of data tuples.

Scalding integrates Cascading within Scala, which includes many functional programming features. The name "Scalding" is a portmanteau of *SCALa* and *cascaDING*. Formally, Scalding is a DSL embedded in Scala that binds to Cascading. A DSL is a language dedicated to a particular kind of problem and solution. The Scala language was designed in part (*http://www.scala-lang.org/node/1403*) to support a wide variety of DSLs. The domain for Scalding is about how to express robust, large-scale data workflows that run on parallel processing frameworks, typically for machine learning use cases.

Avi Bryant, author of Scalding, introduced his talk at the Strata 2012 conference (*http://strataconf.com/stratany2012/public/schedule/detail/25450*) with a special recipe:

> Start on low heat with a base of Hadoop; map, then reduce. Flavor, to taste, with Scala's concise, functional syntax and collections library. Simmer with some Pig bones: a tuple model and high-level join and aggregation operators. Mix in Cascading to hold everything together and boil until it's very, very hot, and you get Scalding, a new API for MapReduce out of Twitter.

> — Avi Bryant
> *Scala + Cascading = Scalding (2012)*

The original release of Scalding was based on a fields-based API (*http://bit.ly/165XiZK*), which is what the examples here use. Subsequently, a type-safe API (*http://bit.ly/14R5vS6*) has been released, although it is currently marked "experimental."

Twitter has released a type-safe Matrix API (*http://bit.ly/10zKtbs*) built on top of Scalding. This provides enormous benefits for the typical kinds of use cases encountered in Scalding. For example, matrix transforms can be used to implement machine learning algorithms that leverage social graph—at very large scale.

Another component is called Algebird (*https://github.com/twitter/algebird*), which is available as an open source project on GitHub.

This library was originally part of the Matrix API but was subsequently promoted into its own project with no dependencies. Algebird provides an abstract algebra library for building aggregation systems. It has excellent uses in streaming algorithms and probabilistic data structures (*http://bit.ly/19YiFUs*), such as Bloom filters (*http://bit.ly/12H01GD*) and Count-Min sketches (*http://bit.ly/1aCUryk*).

Type-safe libraries, efficient operations on large sparse matrices, abstract algebra, etc. —these aspects become particularly important for building distributed algorithms and data services at scale.

Scalding has large-scale commercial deployments at companies such as Twitter, Etsy, eBay, LivePerson, etc. Twitter has many use cases, particularly on the revenue quality team: ad targeting, traffic quality, etc. Etsy had created the JRuby DSL (*http://bit.ly/1aCUx9i*) for Cascading, and now also uses Scalding to perform web analytics and build recommender systems. eBay uses Scalding on its search analytics and other production data pipelines.

Scalding, which was first released in January 2012, won a Bossie 2012 Award from InfoWorld (*http://bit.ly/1b7VAwE*). The award described Scalding as "clean and concise" and "a natural fit":

> Hadoop puts a treasure trove of data at your fingertips, but the process for extracting those riches can be daunting. Cascading provides a thin layer of Java-based data processing functionality atop Hadoop's MapReduce execution layer. It masks the complexity of MapReduce, simplifies the programming, and speeds you on your journey toward actionable analytics. Cascading works with JVM languages like Clojure and JRuby, but we prefer Scalding, a Scala API for Cascading from Twitter. A vast improvement over native MapReduce functions or Pig UDFs, Scalding code is clean and concise. Anyone comfortable with Ruby will find the Cascading/Scala pairing a natural fit.
>
> — James R. Borck
> *InfoWorld magazine (2012)*

In addition to the main Scalding website maintained by Twitter, there are several other excellent resources online:

- Dean Wampler of Think Big Analytics wrote an excellent Scalding tutorial/workshop (*http://bit.ly/19TXJdA*).

- Oscar Boykin of Twitter gave a talk about Scalding at the Hadoop Summit 2012 (*http://slidesha.re/1aCUCK6*).

- Sujit Pal wrote Scalding versions of the "Impatient" series (*http://bit.ly/1b7VJA0*).

- Costin Leau integrated Scalding support into Spring-Hadoop (*http://bit.ly/1b7VK76*).

Books about Scala and Functional Programming

For more information about Scala, DSLs, and functional programming in general, check out these books:

- *DSLs in Action* by Debasish Ghosh (Manning)

- *Functional Programming for Java Developers* by Dean Wampler (O'Reilly)

- *Programming Scala* by Dean Wampler and Alex Payne (O'Reilly)

- *Scala for the Impatient* by Cay Horstmann (Addison-Wesley)

Example 4 in Scalding: Replicated Joins

Next, let's modify the Scalding code to create an app similar to the Cascading version in "Example 4: Replicated Joins" on page 22. We'll show how simple it is to extend pipe assemblies in Scalding.

Starting from the "Impatient" source code directory that you cloned in Git, connect into the *part8* subdirectory. Look at the code in *scripts/scala/Example4.scala*:

```scala
import com.twitter.scalding._

class Example4(args : Args) extends Job(args) {
  val stopPipe = Tsv(args("stop"), ('stop), skipHeader = true)
    .read

  Tsv(args("doc"), ('doc_id, 'text), skipHeader = true)
    .read
    .flatMap('text -> 'token) { text : String => text.split("[ \\[\\]\\(\\),.]") }
    .mapTo('token -> 'token) { token : String => scrub(token) }
    .filter('token) { token : String => token.length > 0 }
    .leftJoinWithTiny('token -> 'stop, stopPipe)
    .filter('stop) { stop : String => stop == null }
    .groupBy('token) { _.size('count) }
    .write(Tsv(args("wc"), writeHeader = true))
```

Example 4 in Scalding: Replicated Joins | 59

```
def scrub(token : String) : String = {
  token
    .trim
    .toLowerCase
}

override def config(implicit mode: Mode): Map[AnyRef, AnyRef] = {
  // resolves "ClassNotFoundException cascading.*" exception on a cluster
  super.config(mode) ++ Map("cascading.app.appjar.class" -> classOf[Example4])
  }
}
```

Only a few lines have changed. First, we add a pipe called stopPipe to read the stop words list. Its tap identifier is specified by a --stop command-line parameter. Note that stopPipe is defined as an immutable variable (read-only) in Scala:

```
val stopPipe = Tsv(args("stop"), ('stop), skipHeader = true)
  .read
```

Next we use a leftJoinWithTiny() function in Scalding to perform the equivalent of a HashJoin in Cascading. This is a replicated join with a left outer join on the stop words. Scalding provides the full set of Join operations (*http://bit.ly/12H0vwl*) provided in Cascading.

After the join, we filter for null values—which is the equivalent of using a RegexFil ter in "Example 4: Replicated Joins":

```
.leftJoinWithTiny('token -> 'stop, stopPipe)
.filter('stop) { stop : String => stop == null }
```

This code is already in the *part8/src/main/scala/* directory, in the *Example4.scala* file. To build and run:

```
$ rm -rf output
$ scald.rb --hdfs-local src/main/scala/Example4.scala \
    --doc data/rain.txt --stop data/en.stop --wc output/wc
```

In the output, the first 10 lines (including the header) should look like this:

```
$ head output/wc/part-00000
token          count
air            1
area           4
australia      1
broken         1
california's   1
cause          1
cloudcover     1
death          1
deserts        1
```

Again, a gist on GitHub (*https://gist.github.com/4371896*) shows building and running this app. If your run looks terribly different, something is probably not set up correctly. Ask the developer community for troubleshooting advice.

In a nutshell, that's how to extend pipe assemblies in Scalding. Welcome to Enterprise data workflows in Scala.

Build Scalding Apps with Gradle

For the example in an upcoming section, we will need to incorporate extensions to Cascading, and the *scald.rb* script will not work for that. Instead, let's look at how to use Gradle to build what is called a "fat jar." In other words, create a JAR file that includes all the class dependencies for Scalding that Apache Hadoop would not normally provide. Note that Gradle version 1.3 or later is required for Scala support.

Starting from the "Impatient" source code directory that you cloned in Git, connect into the *part8* subdirectory. Next, we'll use a Gradle *build.gradle* script to build a Scalding app:

```
apply plugin: 'scala'

archivesBaseName = 'impatient'

repositories {
  mavenLocal()
  mavenCentral()
  mavenRepo name: 'conjars', url: 'http://conjars.org/repo/'
}

dependencies {
  // Scala compiler + related tools, and standard library
  scalaTools 'org.scala-lang:scala-compiler:2.9.2'
  compile 'org.scala-lang:scala-library:2.9.2'

  // Scalding
  compile( 'com.twitter:scalding_2.9.2:0.8.1' )

  // in case you need to add JARs from a local build
  compile fileTree( dir: 'lib', includes: ['*.jar'] )

  compile( 'cascading:cascading-core:2.0.2' )
  compile( 'cascading:cascading-hadoop:2.0.2' )
}

jar {
  description = "Assembles a Hadoop-ready JAR file"
  doFirst {
    into( 'lib' ) {
      from configurations.compile
    }
```

```
  }
  manifest {
    attributes( "Main-Class": "com.twitter.scalding.Tool" )
  }
}
```

Note the `compile( 'com.twitter:scalding_2.9.2:0.8.1' )` directive. This pulls Scalding version 0.8.1 from a Maven repository; check to see if there's a later stable version. Also note that the Cascading version is set to 2.0.2—that's required for the current version of Scalding; again, check to see if that has been bumped up.

This script is already in the *part8/src/main/scala/* directory, in the *build.gradle* file. By the way, if you reuse this script for other projects and ever need to add other JAR files that don't come from Maven repositories—e.g., something built locally—just add them to the *lib* directory.

To verify that your Gradle build for Scalding works properly, let's build and run "Example 3 in Scalding: Word Count with Customized Operations":

```
$ gradle clean jar
$ rm -rf output
$ hadoop jar build/libs/impatient.jar Example3 --hdfs \
    --doc data/rain.txt --wc output/wc
```

Now we can verify the output/wc output:

```
$ head output/wc/part-00000
token        count
a            8
air          1
an           1
and          2
area         4
as           2
australia    1
back         1
broken       1
```

If that output looks correct, you should be good to go. Otherwise, there was probably an issue with the setup. Ask the developer community for troubleshooting advice.

Running on Amazon AWS

We have not yet shown how to run Cascading apps on Hadoop clusters in a cloud, and this Scalding app provides a good example.

To run "Example 3 in Scalding: Word Count with Customized Operations" on the Amazon AWS cloud, first you'll need to have an AWS account set up. Make sure to sign up for EMR, S3, and SimpleDB. Also have your credentials set up in the local configuration —for example, in your *~/.aws_cred/* directory.

Next, install these excellent AWS tools:

s3cmd (http://s3tools.org/s3cmd)
   Create, put, get, delete data in S3

EMR Ruby client (http://aws.amazon.com/developertools/2264)
   Command-line tool for Elastic MapReduce (EMR)

Then edit the *emr.sh* shell script, which is already in the *part8/src/main/scala/* directory —you must update the BUCKET variable to be one of your S3 buckets.

Finally, use the *emr.sh* shell script to upload your JAR plus the input data to S3. That script launches an Apache Hadoop cluster on the Elastic MapReduce (*http://aws.amazon.com/elasticmapreduce/*) service where it runs the app.

```
#!/bin/bash -ex

BUCKET=temp.cascading.org/impatient
NAME=scalding3

# clear previous output
s3cmd del -r s3://$BUCKET/wc

# load built JAR + input data
s3cmd put build/libs/impatient.jar s3://$BUCKET/$NAME.jar
s3cmd put data/rain.txt s3://$BUCKET/rain.txt

# launch cluster and run
elastic-mapreduce --create --name "Scalding" \
  --debug \
  --enable-debugging \
  --log-uri s3n://$BUCKET/logs \
  --jar s3n://$BUCKET/$NAME.jar \
  --arg Example3 \
  --arg "--hdfs" \
  --arg "--doc" \
  --arg s3n://$BUCKET/rain.txt \
  --arg "--wc" \
  --arg s3n://$BUCKET/wc
```

Note that the output path in S3 must be deleted first. Hadoop checks this and will kill a job rather than overwrite an existing data set. Also note how the command-line arguments get passed to EMR through the `--arg` option. Each argument from the Scalding command line must be wrapped. Another nuance is that `s3cmd` uses the usual `s3:` protocol to reference data URIs in S3, whereas the Hadoop jobs running on the EMR service require the `s3n:` protocol. That represents a common reason for job failures on EMR; see also the discussion at the Amazon forums (*http://bit.ly/12H0toj*).

When that `elastic-mapreduce` line executes, it should return a job ID. As the Hadoop job runs on Elastic MapReduce, you can monitor progress in the AWS console based on that job ID. Figure 4-2 shows an example console view for EMR.

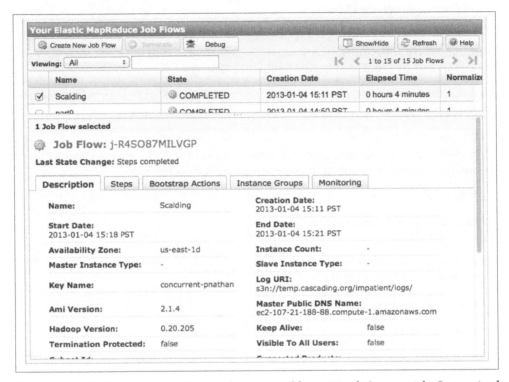

Figure 4-2. EMR console for "Example 3 in Scalding: Word Count with Customized Operations"

After the job completes, check the *wc* directory in the S3 bucket that you used, to confirm results.

## CHAPTER 5

Cascalog—A Clojure DSL for Cascading

Why Use Cascalog?

Sometimes the tools we select change the way we approach a problem. As the proverb goes, if all you have is a hammer, everything looks like a nail. And sometimes our tools, over time, actually interfere with the process of solving a problem.

For most of the past three decades, SQL has been synonymous with database work. A couple of generations of programmers have grown up with relational databases as the de facto standard. Consider that while "NoSQL" has become quite a popular theme, most vendors in the Big Data space have been rushing (circa 2013Q1) to graft SQL features onto their frameworks.

Looking back four decades to the origins of the relational model—in the 1970 paper by Edgar Codd, "A Relational Model of Data for Large Shared Data Banks"—the point was about relational models and not so much about databases and tables and structured queries. Codd himself detested SQL. The relational model was formally specified as a declarative "data sublanguage" (i.e., to be used within some other host language) based on first-order predicate logic (*http://en.wikipedia.org/wiki/Predicate_logic*). SQL is not that. In comparison, it forces programmers to focus largely on control flow issues and the structure of tables—to a much greater extent than the relational model intended. SQL's semantics are also disjoint from the programming languages in which it gets used: Java, C++, Ruby, PHP, etc. For that matter, the term "relational" no longer even appears in the SQL-92 (*http://bit.ly/14R3PYK*) specifications.

Codd's intent, effectively, was to avoid introducing unnecessary complexities that would hamper software systems. He articulated a process for *structuring data* as relations of tuples, as opposed to using structured data that is managed in tables. He also intended queries to be expressed within what we would now call a DSL. Those are subtle points that have enormous implications, which we'll explore in Chapter 7.

Cascalog is a DSL in Clojure (*http://clojure.org/*) that implements first-order predicate logic for large-scale queries based on Cascading. This work originated at a company called BackType, which was subsequently acquired by Twitter.

Clojure is a dialect of Lisp intended for functional programming and parallel processing. The name "Cascalog" is a portmanteau of *CASCading* and *datALOG*. Through the Leiningen build system, you can also run Cascalog in an interpretive prompt called a REPL. This represents a powerful combination, because a developer could test snippets with sample data in a Read-Evaluate-Print Loop (REPL), then compile to a JAR file for production use on a Hadoop cluster.

Getting Started with Cascalog

The best resources for getting started with Cascalog are the project wiki (*https://github.com/nathanmarz/cascalog/wiki*) and API documentation (*http://nathanmarz.github.com/cascalog/*) on GitHub.

In addition to Git and Java, which were set up in Chapter 1, you will need to have a tool called Leiningen installed for the examples in this chapter. Make sure that you have Java 1.6, and then read the steps given on the wiki page (*http://bit.ly/10zL10Y*).

Our example shows using *~/bin* as a target directory for the installation of lein, but you could use any available location on your system:

```
$ export LEIN_HOME=~/bin
$ mkdir -p $LEIN_HOME
$ cd $LEIN_HOME
$ wget https://raw.github.com/technomancy/leiningen/preview/bin/lein
$ chmod 755 lein
$ export PATH=$LEIN_HOME:$PATH
$ export JAVA_OPTS=-Xmx768m
```

That downloads the lein script, makes it executable, and adds it to your PATH environment variable. The script will update itself later.

This provides a build system for Clojure, along with an interactive prompt for evaluating ad hoc queries. Test your installation of lein with the following:

```
$ lein
Leiningen is a tool for working with Clojure projects.
```

There will probably be much more usage text printed out.

Now connect somewhere you have space for downloads, and then use Git to clone the latest update from the master branch of the Cascalog project on GitHub:

```
$ git clone git://github.com/nathanmarz/cascalog.git
```

Connect into that newly cloned directory and run the following steps with lein to get Cascalog set up:

```
$ cd cascalog
$ lein repl
```

That should initiate quite a large number of downloads from the Clojars (*https://clojars.org/*) and Conjars (*http://conjars.org/*) Maven repos. Afterward, you should see an interactive prompt called a REPL:

```
user=>
```

Nathan Marz, the author of Cascalog, wrote an excellent tutorial to introduce the language (*http://bit.ly/12dTR0R*). Let's run through some of those code snippets.

First, load an in-memory data set called playground, which is great to use for simple experimentation:

```
user=> (use 'cascalog.playground) (bootstrap)
nil
nil
user=>
```

Great, that is now loaded into memory. Next, let's run a query:

```
user=> (?<- (stdout) [?person] (age ?person 25))

david
emily
```

Note that many console log lines from Cascading and Apache Hadoop have been redacted—look for the output tuples after a RESULTS line in the console log. The query results david and emily are the persons in the playground data set under age 25. Next let's try a range query:

```
user=> (?<- (stdout) [?person] (age ?person ?age) (< ?age 30))

alice
david
emily
gary
kumar
```

Translated, we have the following:

- The ?<- operator that defines and runs a query
- The query that writes to a sink tap (stdout)
- A list of all matching persons ([?person])
- A generator from the age tap identifier [(age ?person ?age)]
- A predicate that constrains the result set by ?age less than 30

Note that the generator (age ?person ?age) causes the age of each person to be bound to the ?age variable. In Cascalog you specify only what you require, not how it must be achieved. Also, the ordering of predicates is irrelevant. Even though no join operation was specified, this code required an implied join of the person and age data:

```
(def person
  [
   ;; [person]
   ["alice"]
   ["bob"]
   ["chris"]
   ["david"]
   ["emily"]
   ["george"]
   ["gary"]
   ["harold"]
   ["kumar"]
   ["luanne"]
   ])

(def age
  [
   ;; [person age]
   ["alice" 28]
   ["bob" 33]
   ["chris" 40]
   ["david" 25]
   ["emily" 25]
   ["george" 31]
   ["gary" 28]
   ["kumar" 27]
   ["luanne" 36]
   ])
```

Nathan Marz has an excellent tutorial (*http://bit.ly/165YrQR*) about different kinds of joins and filters in Cascalog.

Next let's modify the query to show the age for each person. We simply add the ?age variable to the output tuple scheme:

```
user=> (?<- (stdout) [?person ?age] (age ?person ?age) (< ?age 30))

alice   28
david   25
emily   25
gary    28
kumar   27
```

A gist on GitHub (*https://gist.github.com/4417586*) shows building and running this app. If your results look similar, you should be good to go.

Otherwise, if you have any troubles, contact the Cascalog developer community—which in general is a subset of the Cascading developer community. You can also reach the cascalog-user email forum (*http://bit.ly/12e00dl*) or tweet to #Cascalog on Twitter. Very helpful developers are available to assist.

Example 1 in Cascalog: Simplest Possible App

The tutorial examples show Cascalog code snippets run in the interactive REPL. Next let's use lein to build a "fat jar" that can also run on an Apache Hadoop cluster.

Paul Lam of uSwitch has translated each of the "Impatient" series of Cascading apps into Cascalog, some of which are more expressive than the originals (*https://github.com/Quantisan/Impatient/wiki*).

Connect somewhere you have space for downloads, and then use Git to clone the Cascalog version of "Impatient" on GitHub:

```
$ git clone git://github.com/Quantisan/Impatient.git
```

Connect into the *part8* subdirectory. Then we'll review an app in Cascalog for a distributed file copy, similar to "Example 1: Simplest Possible App in Cascading" on page 3:

```
cd Impatient/part1
```

Source is located in the *src/impatient/core.clj* file:

```
(ns impatient.core
  (:use [cascalog.api]
        [cascalog.more-taps :only (hfs-delimited)])
  (:gen-class))

(defn -main [in out & args]
  (?<- (hfs-delimited out)
       [?doc ?line]
       ((hfs-delimited in :skip-header? true) ?doc ?line)))
```

The first four lines, which begin with a macro ns, define a namespace (*http://clojure.org/namespaces*). Java and Scala use packages and imports for similar reasons, but in general Clojure namespaces are more advanced. For example, they provide better features for avoiding naming collisions. Namespaces are also first-class constructs in Clojure, so they can be composed dynamically. In this example, the namespace imports the Cascalog API, plus additional definitions for Cascading taps—such as TextDelimited for TSV format.

The next four lines, which begin with a macro defn, define a function (*http://clojure.org/functional_programming*), which is analogous to the Main method in "Example 1: Simplest Possible App in Cascading". It has arguments for the in source tap identifier and the out sink tap identifier, plus an args argument list for arity overloading. A query writes output in TSV format for each tuple of ?doc and ?line fields from the input tuple

Example 1 in Cascalog: Simplest Possible App | 69

stream. Note the property `:skip-header?` set to `true`, which causes the source tap to skip headers in the input TSV data.

Next we compile and build to create a "fat jar." This packages up all the project files and dependencies into a single JAR file. Dependencies are defined in the *project.clj* build script:

```
(defproject impatient "0.1.0-SNAPSHOT"
  :description "Cascalog for the Impatient - Part 1"
  :url "https://github.com/Quantisan/Impatient/tree/cascalog/part1"
  :license {:name "Eclipse Public License"
            :url "http://www.eclipse.org/legal/epl-v10.html"}
  :uberjar-name "impatient.jar"
  :aot [impatient.core]
  :main impatient.core
  :dependencies [[org.clojure/clojure "1.4.0"]
                 [cascalog "1.10.0"]
                 [cascalog-more-taps "0.3.0"]]
  :profiles {:provided {:dependencies \
  [[org.apache.hadoop/hadoop-core "0.20.2-dev"]]}})
```

Note that this build script is written in Clojure. For detailed descriptions of all the configuration options available in a *project.clj* script, see the annotated sample (*https:// github.com/technomancy/leiningen/blob/stable/sample.project.clj*).

Given the range and complexities of JVM-based build systems—Maven, Ivy, Gradle, Ant, SBT, etc.—navigating through a build script is perhaps the single biggest hurdle encountered when programmers start to learn about these frameworks. Clojure and Leiningen make this essential concern quite simple. No surprises. The build is written in the language.

To build with `lein`:

```
$ lein clean
$ lein uberjar
Created /Users/ceteri/opt/Impatient/part1/target/impatient.jar
```

The resulting JAR should now be located at *target/impatient.jar* with everything needed for Hadoop standalone mode. To run it:

```
$ rm -rf output
$ hadoop jar ./target/impatient.jar data/rain.txt output/rain
```

Take a look at the output in the *output/rain/part-00000* partition file. It should be the same as for "Example 1: Simplest Possible App in Cascading". Again, a gist on Git-Hub (*https://gist.github.com/4417586*) shows a log of this.

Example 4 in Cascalog: Replicated Joins

Next, let's review the Cascalog code for an app similar to the Cascading version in "Example 4: Replicated Joins" on page 22. Starting from the "Impatient" source code directory that you cloned in Git, connect into the *part4* subdirectory. Look at the code in *src/impatient/core.clj*:

```
(ns impatient.core
  (:use [cascalog.api]
        [cascalog.more-taps :only (hfs-delimited)])
  (:require [clojure.string :as s]
            [cascalog.ops :as c])
  (:gen-class))

(defmapcatop split [line]
  "reads in a line of string and splits it by regex"
  (s/split line #"[\[\]\\\(\),.)\s]+"))

(defn -main [in out stop & args]
  (let [rain (hfs-delimited in :skip-header? true)
        stop (hfs-delimited stop :skip-header? true)]
    (?<- (hfs-delimited out)
         [?word ?count]
         (rain _ ?line)
         (split ?line :> ?word-dirty)
         ((c/comp s/trim s/lower-case) ?word-dirty :> ?word)
         (stop ?word :> false)
         (c/count ?count))))
```

Again, this begins with a namespace, which serves as the target of a compilation (*http://clojure.org/compilation*). This namespace also imports the Clojure string library (denoted by an s/ prefix) plus the Cascalog aggregator operations (denoted by a c/ prefix).

Next there is a defmapcatop macro that defines a split operation to split text lines into a token output stream—effectively a generator. This is based on a regex function in the Clojure string library.

Next there is the main definition, similar to "Example 1: Simplest Possible App in Cascading", which now includes a stop source tap identifier to read the stop words list:

- Define and run a query.
- Write output tuples to the out sink tap, in TSV format.
- Output tuple scheme has ?word and ?count fields.
- Generator from the rain source tap identifier, in TSV format.
- Input tuple scheme uses only the ?line field; the _ ignores the first field.

Example 4 in Cascalog: Replicated Joins | 71

- Each line is split into tokens, represented by the ?word-dirty variable.

- A composition c/comp performs a string trim and converts the token represented by ?word to lowercase.

- The stop data filters out matched tokens, implying a left join.

- An aggregator c/count counts each token, represented by ?count.

It's interesting that the Cascalog code for the Replicated Joins example is actually longer than its Scalding equivalent. Even so, in Scalding much more of the "how"—the imperative programming aspects—must be articulated. For example, the join, aggregation, and filters in the Scalding version are more explicit. Also, to be fair, writing those Scalding examples took some effort to find approaches that conformed to Scala requirements for the pipes.

Figure 5-1 shows the conceptual flow diagram for "Example 4: Replicated Joins". Note that here in the Cascalog version, there is no "pipeline" per se. The workflow is exactly the definition of the main function. Whereas the Scalding code provides an almost pure expression of the Cascading flow, the Cascalog version expresses the desired end goal of the workflow with less imperative "controls" defined. For example, the GroupBy is not needed. Again, in Cascalog you specify what is required, not how it must be achieved.

To build:

```
$ lein clean
$ lein uberjar
Created /Users/ceteri/opt/Impatient/part4/target/impatient.jar
```

To run:

```
$ rm -rf output
$ hadoop jar ./target/impatient.jar data/rain.txt output/wc data/en.stop
```

To verify:

```
$ cat output/wc/part-00000
```

The results should be the same as in the Cascading version ("Example 4: Replicated Joins").

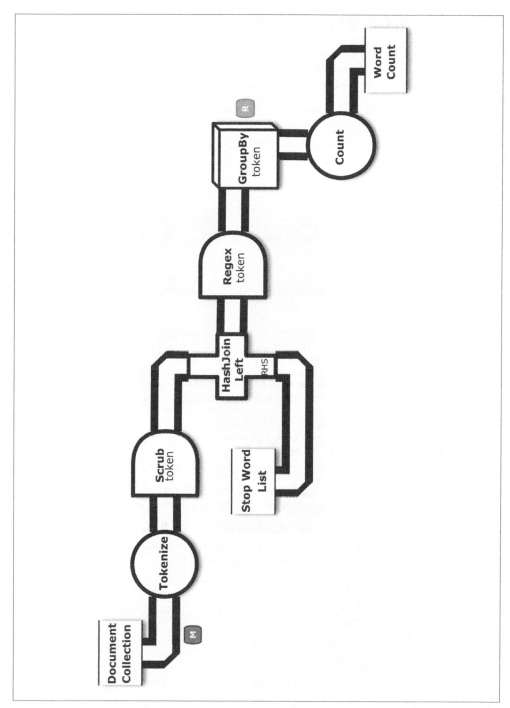

Figure 5-1. Conceptual flow diagram for "Example 4: Replicated Joins"

Example 4 in Cascalog: Replicated Joins | 73

Example 6 in Cascalog: TF-IDF with Testing

The TF-IDF with Testing example in Cascalog by Paul Lam is brilliant. It uses approximately 70 lines of Cascalog code, versus approximately 180 lines of Cascading (Java). Plus, the Cascalog version is much simpler to follow.

Starting from the "Impatient" source code directory that you cloned in Git, connect into the *part6* subdirectory. Look at the code in *src/impatient/core.clj*, starting with the namespace and definitions we used earlier in "Example 4 in Cascalog: Replicated Joins":

```
(ns impatient.core
  (:use [cascalog.api]
        [cascalog.checkpoint]
        [cascalog.more-taps :only (hfs-delimited)])
  (:require [clojure.string :as s]
            [cascalog [ops :as c] [vars :as v]])
  (:gen-class))

(defmapcatop split [line]
  "reads in a line of string and splits it by regex"
  (s/split line #"[\[\]\\\(\),.)\s]+"))

(defn scrub-text [s]
  "trim open whitespaces and lower case"
  ((comp s/trim s/lower-case) s))
```

Great, those are essentially the same as in the earlier example. The next two definitions create the stream assertion used to drop badly formed input tuples:

```
(defn assert-tuple [pred msg x]
  "helper function to add assertion to tuple stream"
  (when (nil? (assert (pred x) msg))
    true))

(def assert-doc-id ^{:doc "assert doc-id is correct format"}
  (partial assert-tuple #(re-seq #"doc\d+" %) "unexpected doc-id"))
```

The remainder of the app is divided into three subqueries: ETL, Word Count, and TF-IDF. First comes the ETL subquery, which loads input, tokenizes lines of text, filters stop words, applies the stream assertion, and binds a failure trap:

```
(defn etl-docs-gen [rain stop]
  (<- [?doc-id ?word]
      (rain ?doc-id ?line)
      (split ?line :> ?word-dirty)
      (scrub-text ?word-dirty :> ?word)
      (stop ?word :> false)
      (assert-doc-id ?doc-id)
      (:trap (hfs-textline "output/trap" :sinkmode :update))))
```

Next we have the Word Count functionality from before, now as a simplified subquery because it follows immediately after the point where the text lines get tokenized:

```
(defn word-count [src]
  "simple word count across all documents"
  (<- [?word ?count]
      (src _ ?word)
      (c/count ?count)))
```

Next we have functions for the three branches, "D," "DF," and "TF." Note that in Cascalog a branch is defined as a function—to some extent, this reinforces the concept of *closures* in functional programming, at least much better than could be performed in Java.

A similar construct was also leveraged in the failure trap used in the stream assertion, for the etl-docs-gen subquery. In Cascading, branch names get propagated through a pipe assembly, then used in a flow definition to bind failure traps. The specification of a failure trap gets dispersed through different portions of a Cascading app. In contrast, Cascalog has branches and traps specified concisely within a function definition, as first-class language constructs.

```
(defn D [src]
  (let [src (select-fields src ["?doc-id"])]
    (<- [?n-docs]
        (src ?doc-id)
        (c/distinct-count ?doc-id :> ?n-docs))))

(defn DF [src]
  (<- [?df-word ?df-count]
      (src ?doc-id ?df word)
      (c/distinct-count ?doc-id ?df-word :> ?df-count)))

(defn TF [src]
  (<- [?doc-id ?tf-word ?tf-count]
      (src ?doc-id ?tf-word)
      (c/count ?tf-count)))
```

Note the use of another Cascalog aggregator, the c/distinct-count function. This is equivalent to the Unique filter in Cascading.

Next we construct two definitions to calculate TF-IDF. The first is the actual formula, which shows how to use math functions. It also uses a Clojure threading operator ->> for caching the query results in memory.

The second definition is the function for the "TF-IDF" branch, which implies the joins needed for the "D," "DF," and "TF" branches.

```
(defn tf-idf-formula [tf-count df-count n-docs]
  (->> (+ 1.0 df-count)
       (div n-docs)
       (Math/log)
       (* tf-count)))

(defn TF-IDF [src]
  (let [n-doc (first (flatten (??- (D src))))]
```

Example 6 in Cascalog: TF-IDF with Testing | 75

```
(<- [?doc-id ?tf-idf ?tf-word]
    ((TF src) ?doc-id ?tf-word ?tf-count)
    ((DF src) ?tf-word ?df-count)
    (tf-idf-formula ?tf-count ?df-count n-doc :> ?tf-idf))))
```

Last, we have the `main` function, which handles the command-line arguments for the tap identifiers. Notice that it uses a `workflow` macro, which is an important construct in Cascalog. The workflow macro, authored by Sam Ritchie at Twitter, is described in detail at his GitHub site (*http://bit.ly/12dTWl6*).

"Example 6 in Cascalog: TF-IDF with Testing" calculates TF-IDF metrics by abstracting the problem into subqueries. Each step within the workflow is named, and as a collection these steps represent the required subqueries for the app:

etl-step
> The ETF subquery

tf-step
> The TF-IDF subquery

wrd-step
> The Word Count subquery

The `main` function is a collection of these three subqueries:

```
(defn -main [in out stop tfidf & args]
  (workflow
    ["tmp/checkpoint"]
    etl-step ([:tmp-dirs etl-stage]
              (let [rain (hfs-delimited in :skip-header? true)
                    stop (hfs-delimited stop :skip-header? true)]
                (?- (hfs-delimited etl-stage)
                    (etl-docs-gen rain stop))))
    tf-step  ([:deps etl-step]
              (let [src (name-vars (hfs-delimited etl-stage :skip-header? true)
                                   ["?doc-id" "?word"])]
                (?- (hfs-delimited tfidf)
                    (TF-IDF src))))
    wrd-step ([:deps etl-step]
              (?- (hfs-delimited out)
                  (word-count (hfs-delimited etl-stage))))))
```

The workflow is a first-class construct in Cascalog, unlike in Cascading or Scalding, where workflows get inferred from the pipe assemblies. The steps each list their dependencies, and the steps may run in parallel if they are independent. To be clear, recognize that this term "step" is quite different from an Apache Hadoop job step.

Instead the Cascalog step is used for checkpoints, which are built directly into workflows. Notice the definition `["tmp/checkpoint"]` just before the first step. That specifies a location for checkpointed data. If any steps cause the app to fail, then when you resubmit the app, the workflow macro will skip all the steps preceding the point of failure.

To build:

```
$ lein clean
$ lein uberjar
Created /Users/ceteri/opt/Impatient/part6/target/impatient.jar
```

To run:

```
$ rm -rf output
$ hadoop jar target/impatient.jar data/rain.txt output/wc \
    data/en.stop output/tfidf
```

To verify the output:

```
$ cat output/trap/part-m-00001-00001
zoink
$ head output/tfidf/part-00000
doc02   0.22314355131420976     area
doc01   0.44628710262841953     area
doc03   0.22314355131420976     area
doc05   0.9162907318741551      australia
doc05   0.9162907318741551      broken
doc04   0.9162907318741551      california's
doc04   0.9162907318741551      cause
doc02   0.9162907318741551      cloudcover
doc04   0.9162907318741551      death
doc04   0.9162907318741551      deserts
```

"Example 6 in Cascalog: TF-IDF with Testing" also includes unit tests, with source code in the *test/impatient/core_test.clj* file:

```
(ns impatient.core-test
  (:use impatient.core
        clojure.test
        cascalog.api
        [midje sweet cascalog]))

(deftest scrub-text-test
  (fact
    (scrub-text "FoO BAR  ") => "foo bar"))

(deftest etl-docs-gen-test
  (let [rain [["doc1" "a b c"]]
        stop [["b"]]]
    (fact
      (etl-docs-gen rain stop) => (produces [["doc1" "a"]
                                             ["doc1" "c"]]))))
```

Note the reference to midje in the namespace. These tests are based on a test framework called Midje-Cascalog, described by Ritchie on his GitHub project (*https://github.com/sritchie/midje-cascalog*) and in substantially more detail in his article about best practices for Cascalog testing (*http://sritchie.github.io/2012/01/22/cascalog-testing-20/*).

Example 6 in Cascalog: TF-IDF with Testing | 77

Midje enables you to test Cascalog queries as functions, whether they are isolated or within part of a workflow. Each test definition shown in the preceding code uses `fact` to make a statement about a query and its expected results. These tests duplicate the unit tests that were used in "Example 6: TF-IDF with Testing" on page 41. Midje also has features for stubs and mocks. Ritchie explains how Midje in Cascalog represents a game-changer for testing MapReduce apps:

> Without proper tests, Hadoop developers can't help but be scared of making changes to production code. When creativity might bring down a workflow, it's easiest to get it working once and leave it alone.[1]
>
> This approach is not just better than the *state of the art* of MapReduce testing, as defined by Cloudera; it completely obliterates the old way of thinking, and makes it possible to build very complex workflows with a minimum of uncertainty.[2]

> — Sam Ritchie

Incorporating TDD, assertions, traps, and checkpoints into the Cascalog workflow macro was sheer brilliance, for Enterprise data workflows done right. Moreover, fact-based tests separate a Cascalog app's logic from concerns about how its data is stored—reducing the complexity of required testing.

To run the tests for "Example 6 in Cascalog: TF-IDF with Testing":

```
$ lein test
Retrieving org/clojure/clojure/maven-metadata.xml (2k)
    from http://repo1.maven.org/maven2/
Retrieving org/clojure/clojure/maven-metadata.xml (1k)
    from https://clojars.org/repo/
Retrieving org/clojure/clojure/maven-metadata.xml (2k)
    from http://repo1.maven.org/maven2/
Retrieving org/clojure/clojure/maven-metadata.xml
    from http://oss.sonatype.org/content/repositories/snapshots/
Retrieving org/clojure/clojure/maven-metadata.xml
    from http://oss.sonatype.org/content/repositories/releases/

lein test impatient.core-test

Ran 2 tests containing 2 assertions.
0 failures, 0 errors.
```

Again, a gist on GitHub (*https://gist.github.com/4417586*) shows a log of this run.

Cascalog Technology and Uses

A common critique from programmers who aren't familiar with Clojure is that they would need to learn Lisp. Actually, the real learning curve for Cascalog is more often

---

1. *http://sritchie.github.io/2011/09/30/testing-cascalog-with-midje/*
2. *http://sritchie.github.io/2011/09/29/getting-creative-with-mapreduce/*

the need to learn Prolog. Datalog (*http://en.wikipedia.org/wiki/Datalog*) is formally a subset of Prolog (*http://en.wikipedia.org/wiki/Prolog*)—in terms of its syntax.

Unlike Prolog, however, Datalog represents a truly declarative logic programming language: it expresses the logic for a unit of work without needing to specify its control flow. This is great for query languages, and Datalog did influence "recursive queries" in Oracle, "Magic Sets" in DB2, etc. Declarative logic programming is also the basis for specifying "what" is needed instead of "how" it must be achieved. Within the context of a functional programming paradigm—and especially within the context of Cascading workflows and parallel processing—many decisions about "how" can be deferred to the flow planner to leverage the underlying topology.

Cascalog leverages Datalog and Cascading within Clojure to provide several key benefits:

- Code is very compact, generally smaller than with other Hadoop abstraction layers.
- An interactive REPL makes development and testing convenient and efficient.
- Generating queries dynamically is easy and idiomatic—unlike in SQL.
- Interspersing queries within the rest of the application logic is trivial—unlike in Java + SQL.
- Custom operations get defined just like any other function—unlike the UDFs used in Hive, Pig, etc.

An interesting aspect of having the REPL is that Cascalog provides many of the benefits of Apache Hive—convenient for ad hoc queries, roll-ups, etc. However, the queries are more expressive than SQL and, in general, an order of magnitude less code is required for comparable Cascalog apps. Meanwhile, Cascalog apps provide deterministic workflows within a functional programming paradigm. Apache Hive does not.

There are a number of published articles and case studies about large-scale commercial deployments of Cascalog. Nathan Marz authored the language while working at Back-Type, which was subsequently acquired by Twitter. The publisher analytics team at Twitter uses Cascalog apps at very large scale for ETL, ad hoc queries, predictive modeling, etc.

Other interesting deployments include:

The Climate Corporation (http://climate.com/)
    Insuring farmers against crop losses due to global warming

Nokia (http://m.maps.nokia.com/)
    Location services, mobile maps, etc.

uSwitch (http://www.uswitch.com/)
    Price comparison and switching

Factual (http://blog.factual.com/clojure-on-hadoop-a-new-hope)
 Geolocation data sets

Harvard School of Public Health (http://bit.ly/120Z5lh)
 Next-generation gene sequencing

Yieldbot (http://www.yieldbot.com/)
 Real-time customer intent for advertising

Linkfluence (http://us.linkfluence.net/)
 Preparing social graph data sets prior to analysis in Gephi or Neo4j

Lumosity (http://www.lumosity.com/)
 Data analytics for R&D in cognitive enhancement

Books about Cascalog and Clojure

For more information about Cascalog and Clojure programming in general, check out these books:

- *Big Data* by Nathan Marz and James Warren (Manning)
- *Clojure Programming* by Chas Emerick, Brian Carper, and Christophe Grand (O'Reilly)
- *Practical Clojure* by Luke VanderHart and Stuart Sierra (Apress)

While preparing code samples for this book, the build systems used for Cascading, Scalding, and Cascalog showed some contrasts. Scalding scripts used `sbt`, Gradle, and Maven. Simple tasks were simple to perform, but more complicated work required troubleshooting, digging through manuals, workarounds, etc. In contrast, developing the Cascalog examples with `lein` was amazingly straightforward. On the one hand, preferences for programming languages vary widely between individuals and organizations, and many people find that the Lisp syntax in Clojure is difficult to understand. On the other hand, you'll need to search far and wide to find many complaints about Leiningen.

## CHAPTER 6

Beyond MapReduce

Applications and Organizations

Overall, the notion of an Enterprise data workflow spans well beyond Hadoop, integrating many different kinds of frameworks and processes. Consider the architecture in Figure 6-1 as a strawman that shows where a typical Enterprise data workflow runs.

In the center there is a workflow consuming from some unstructured data—most likely some kind of machine data, such as log files—plus some other, more structured data from another framework, such as customer profiles. That workflow runs on an Apache Hadoop cluster, and possibly on other topologies, such as in-memory data grids (IMDGs).

Some of the results go directly to a frontend use case, such as getting pushed into Memcached, which is backing a customer API. Line of business use cases are what drive most of the need for Big Data apps.

Some of the results also go to the back office. Enterprise organizations almost always have made substantial investments in data infrastructure for the back office, in the process used to integrate systems and coordinate different departments, and in the people trained in that process. Workflow results such as data cubes get pushed from the Hadoop cluster out to an analytics framework. In turn, those data cubes get consumed for reporting needs, data science work, customer support, etc.

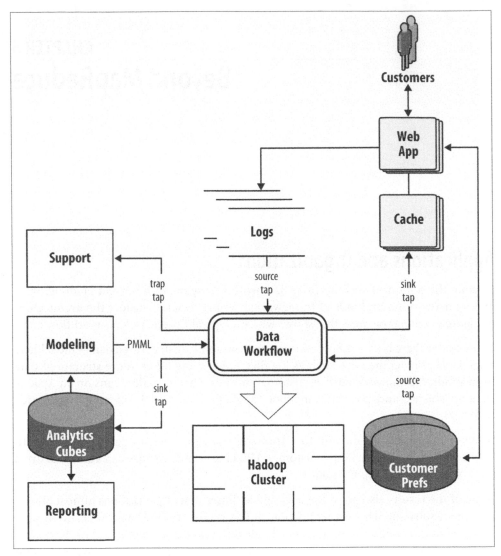

Figure 6-1. Strawman workflow architecture

We can also view this strawman workflow from a functional perspective at Enterprise scale, shown in Figure 6-2.

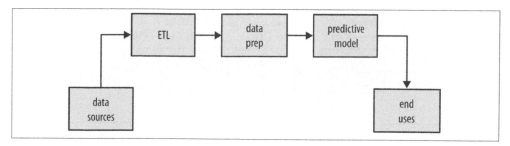

Figure 6-2. Strawman—units of work

Different departments are typically responsible for specific units of work. Multiple data sources get loaded and merged through the ETL process. Many organizations perform that ETL within a data warehouse, such as Teradata, where the unit of work is defined in ANSI SQL queries. Most use cases require additional data preparation, applying business logic that is specific to an organization—for example, cleaning the data and producing sample training sets. Apache Pig is a popular tool for that kind of data preparation on a Hadoop cluster. Those data sets may get used to create and score predictive models: classifiers, recommenders, forecasts, etc. Many organizations perform their modeling within an analytics framework, such as SAS. Application developers translate specifications from the analysts' models into another programming language, such as Java, to run at scale. Then the data products from those apps must be integrated into end use cases.

At this point, the business process for our strawman app has probably crossed through four or five departments: Ops, Analytics, plus a few different applications teams. And while some organizations have adopted more of Data Science practice—introducing multidisciplinary teams that can handle all of those functions—in reality, most Enterprise firms will have these responsibilities split across different departments, probably with each team leveraging different frameworks. That creates an issue of operational complexity, because the business process for the workflow is defined and executed in pieces. Ops ultimately has responsibility for keeping the entire workflow running smoothly, even though it crosses several boundaries; part of it gets defined in ANSI SQL, part in Pig, part in SAS, part in Java, etc.

This kind of problem is why Enterprise organizations leverage Cascading. The entire business process can be defined in one app—one JAR file—that integrates each of the respective units of work, as shown in Figure 6-3. Rather than translating requirements from each department into Java, Clojure, Scala, etc., most of the work can be integrated directly.

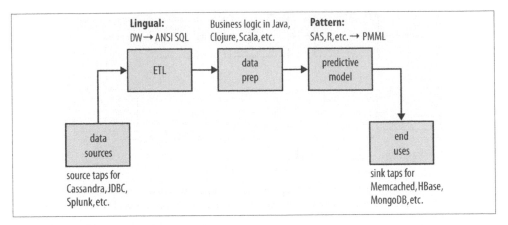

Figure 6-3. Strawman—functional integration

To support this, Cascading includes two components, Lingual for ANSI SQL and Pattern for PMML, which are effectively DSLs. These allow for all of the following:

- ETL, which has been run in ANSI SQL, can be used directly in Lingual flows.
- Data preparation can be handled in Cascading, Cascalog, Scalding, etc.
- Predictive models can be exported as PMML and used directly in Pattern flows, for scoring at scale.
- Cascading taps integrate other frameworks for the data sources and sinks.
- All of this goes into one app, one JAR, which Ops can schedule and instrument with much less complexity.
- Some optimizations may become possible for the flow planners and compiler as a result of this integration.

In other words, the different departments have a way to collaborate on a combined app that ties together and optimizes business processes across the organization.

Lingual, a DSL for ANSI SQL

Lingual is an extension to Cascading that executes ANSI SQL (*http://en.wikipedia.org/wiki/SQL-92*) queries as Cascading apps. This open source project is a collaboration between Cascading and Optiq (*https://github.com/julianhyde/optiq*)—an ANSI-compliant SQL parser/optimizer written by Julian Hyde, the author of Mondrian (*http://mondrian.pentaho.com/*). Julian wrote a good description of the project (*http://julianhyde.blogspot.com/2013/02/announcing-lingual.html*).

It is important to note that Lingual itself is not a database. Rather, it leverages the power of SQL to describe the business logic for data workflows—as a kind of functional programming. In that sense Lingual implements a domain-specific language (DSL) where Cascading workflows get defined in SQL. Optiq provides compatibility with a wide range of commercial implementations for ANSI SQL: tested with more than 6,000 complex SQL statements from production queries in DB2, Oracle, Teradata, SQL Server, etc.

Consider that ANSI SQL provides the lingua franca for describing data in Enterprise. People working in data management often think of *database*, *relational*, and *SQL* as all referring to the same thing. In reality, most of the databases in use today are non-relational; e.g., banking makes enormous use of hierarchical databases. Moreover, SQL is not quite the same as the relational model. Edgar Codd, the author of the relational model, spent much of the latter part of his career arguing that point. However, SQL is a language—a declarative language, mostly based on a functional programming paradigm—and it describes workflows that are directed acyclic graphs (DAGs). In that sense, SQL corresponds quite closely to the internals of Cascading.

Another subtle point is that Lingual is not intended for low-latency, ad hoc queries. In that sense it is the opposite of "SQL on Hadoop" platforms such as Apache Hive—where people issue queries and expect rapid responses. Instead, Lingual provides for high-throughput work. Studies based on many years of Enterprise SQL use case analysis have shown a long tail of machine-to-machine batch processing. In other words, a mission-critical business process gets defined in SQL, with queries written by a machine.

ETL is a typical use case for this in Enterprise. On the one hand, large-scale joins, filtering, and aggregation are typically required. On the other hand, the source data is probably not indexed and almost certainly not normalized. The requirements for ETL are nearly the opposite of what a relational database provides. Many of the Enterprise deployments of Cascading apps are ETL—addressing complex data quality problems that are readily handled by the "plumbing" of traps, flows, branches, merges, etc.

Using the SQL Command Shell

In addition to the Lingual library and a JAR file used to build Cascading apps, other components include the following:

- SQL command shell
- Catalog manager
- JDBC driver

To install the SQL command shell, run the following script:

```
$ curl \
  http://files.concurrentinc.com/lingual/1.0/lingual-client/ \
  install-lingual-client.sh | bash
```

That will create a *~/.lingual-client/* directory, which needs to be added to your PATH environment variable.

```
$ export PATH=~/.lingual-client/bin/:$PATH
```

When using Lingual with Apache Hadoop, the SQL command shell expects certain environment variables to be set. That way the correct Hadoop version and configuration will be included in the CLASSPATH:

HADOOP_HOME
    Path to local Hadoop installation

HADOOP_CONF_DIR
    Defaults to *$HADOOP_HOME/conf*

HADOOP_USER_NAME
    The username to use when submitting Hadoop jobs

Assuming that you have HADOOP_HOME already set, then:

```
$ export HADOOP_CONF_DIR=$HADOOP_HOME/conf
$ export HADOOP_USER_NAME=<username>
```

If you're working with a remote Elastic MapReduce (*http://aws.amazon.com/elastic mapreduce/*) cluster on Amazon AWS, see the Bash EMR (*https://github.com/cwensel/ bash-emr*) utilities. Specifically, use the emrconf command to fetch remote configuration files.

If you encounter errors executing SQL queries on a remote cluster (Amazon AWS, Windows Azure HDInsight, etc.) try the following workaround:

```
$ export HADOOP_USER_NAME=hadoop
```

That should resolve security issues that may be causing failures on the remote cluster.

Now let's try using the Lingual SQL command shell. The following example is based on data from the MySQL Sample Employee Database (*http://launchpad.net/test-db*):

```
$ mkdir -p ~/src/lingual
$ cd ~/src/lingual
$ curl http://data.cascading.org/employees.tgz | tar xvz
```

That creates an *employees* subdirectory for the table data, which is essentially several large CSV files. Next, load the schema for these tables into Lingual using SQL data definitions:

```
$ curl http://data.cascading.org/create-employees.sh > create-employees.sh
$ chmod +x ./create-employees.sh
$ ./create-employees.sh local
```

Now try the SQL command line, querying to show a relational catalog for these tables:

```
$ lingual shell
0: jdbc:lingual:local> !tables
```

That lists metadata about the available tables: EMPLOYEE, TITLES, SALARIES. Next, let's try a simple query:

```
0: jdbc:lingual:local> SELECT * FROM EMPLOYEES.EMPLOYEES WHERE FIRST_NAME = 'Gina';
```

The result set should show records for a whole bunch of people named Gina.

An interesting use case for the Lingual SQL command shell is in organizations that use Hadoop for large-scale data products, which are not using SQL already. For example, consider the case where an Engineering team is building machine learning apps in Cascalog…then Customer Support comes along with an interrupt task to pull the data for a particular customer ID. Rather than derail Engineering with Support interrupts, it makes sense to expose a view of the data through standard tools with ANSI SQL and JDBC connections—these will already be familiar to the people working in Support, Finance, Ops, etc.

Using the JDBC Driver

Connect to a directory on your computer where you have a few gigabytes of available disk space, and then clone the source code repo from GitHub:

```
$ git clone git://github.com/Cascading/lingual.git
```

Once that completes, connect into the *lingual* directory, then into the *lingual-local* subdirectory. Next build the Lingual JDBC connector to run locally:

```
$ gradle clean fatjar
```

Then connect into the *../lingual-examples* subdirectory and take a look at the *src/main/java/cascading/lingual/examples/foodmart/JdbcExample.java* app. Java source used to execute SQL queries through a Lingual JDBC connection is much the same as with any other JDBC driver:

```java
import java.sql.Connection;
import java.sql.DriverManager;
import java.sql.ResultSet;
import java.sql.SQLException;
import java.sql.Statement;

public class JdbcExample
  {
  public static void main( String[] args ) throws Exception
    {
    new JdbcExample().run();
    }

  public void run() throws ClassNotFoundException, SQLException
    {
```

```java
Class.forName( "cascading.lingual.jdbc.Driver" );
Connection connection = DriverManager.getConnection(
    "jdbc:lingual:local;schemas=src/main/resources/data/example" );
Statement statement = connection.createStatement();

ResultSet resultSet = statement.executeQuery(
    "select *\n"
    + "from \"example\".\"sales_fact_1997\" as s\n"
    + "join \"example\".\"employee\" as e\n"
    + "on e.\"EMPID\" = s.\"CUST_ID\"" );

while( resultSet.next() )
  {
  int n = resultSet.getMetaData().getColumnCount();
  StringBuilder builder = new StringBuilder();

  for( int i = 1; i <= n; i++ )
    {
    builder.append(( i > 1 ? "; " : "" )
        + resultSet.getMetaData().getColumnLabel( i )
        + "="
        + resultSet.getObject( i ) );
    }

  System.out.println( builder );
    }

resultSet.close();
statement.close();
connection.close();
  }
}
```

In this example, the table schema gets derived directly from the headers of the CSV files. In other words, point a JDBC connection at a directory of flat files and query them as tables—as if they had already been loaded into a SQL database—without needing the database.

To build and run the JDBC example:

```
$ gradle clean jar
$ hadoop jar build/libs/lingual-examples-1.0.0-wip-dev.jar
```

This sample app uses Lingual to open a JDBC connection and run the following SQL query:

```sql
SELECT *
  FROM "example"."sales_fact_1997" AS s
  JOIN "example"."employee" AS e
    ON e."EMPID" = s."CUST_ID"
;
```

Keep in mind that the quote marks are important, and table names are case-sensitive on some operating systems (this is due to Java).

The query runs on example data in the *src/main/resources/data/example/* subdirectory in the CSV files there. Query results should look like this:

```
CUST_ID=100; PROD_ID=10; EMPID=100; NAME=Bill
CUST_ID=150; PROD_ID=20; EMPID=150; NAME=Sebastian
```

It's interesting to consider how the code would look in an equivalent Cascading app:

```
Tap empTap =
  new FileTap(new TextDelimited(true, ",", "\""), "src/test/data/employee.txt");
Tap salesTap =
  new FileTap(new TextDelimited(true, ",", "\""), "src/test/data/salesfact.txt");

Tap resultsTap =
  new FileTap(new TextDelimited(true, ",", "\""), "build/test/output/results.txt",
  SinkMode.REPLACE);

Pipe empPipe = new Pipe("emp");
Pipe salesPipe = new Pipe("sales");

Pipe join =
  new CoGroup(empPipe, new Fields("empid"), salesPipe, new Fields("cust_id"));

FlowDef flowDef = flowDef()
    .setName("flow")
    .addSource(empPipe, empTap)
    .addSource(salesPipe, salesTap)
    .addTailSink(join, resultsTap);

Flow flow = new LocalFlowConnector().connect(flowDef);
flow.start();

TupleEntryIterator iterator = resultTap.openForRead();
```

Arguably, that code is more compact than the JDBC use case. Even so, Lingual allows for Cascading apps that read SQL queries as flat files, as command-line options—which can leverage a great number of existing ANSI SQL queries.

Integrating with Desktop Tools

By virtue of having a JDBC connector into Cascading workflows on Apache Hadoop clusters, we can leverage many existing SQL tools. For example, Toad (*http://www.toad world.com/*) is a popular tool for interacting with SQL frameworks. RStudio (*http://www.rstudio.com/*) (shown in Figure 6-4) is a popular IDE for statistical computing in R, which can import data through JDBC.

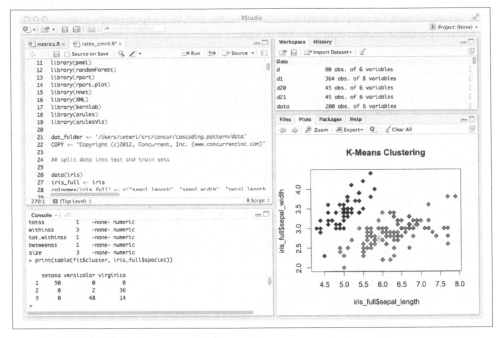

Figure 6-4. RStudio

The following example is based on the RJDBC (*http://www.rforge.net/RJDBC/*) package for R, assuming that the *MySQL Sample Employee Database* has been downloaded as described previously. This illustrates a common use case for embedded SQL queries leveraging unstructured data, i.e., the long tail of machine-to-machine communications:

```
# JDBC support in R is provided by the RJDBC package http://www.rforge.net/RJDBC/
# install the RJDBC package; only needed once--uncomment next line the first time
#install.packages("RJDBC", dep=TRUE)

# load the library
library(RJDBC)

# set up the driver
drv <- JDBC("cascading.lingual.jdbc.Driver",
  "~/src/concur/lingual/lingual-local/build/libs/
  lingual-local-1.0.0-wip-dev-jdbc.jar")

# set up a database connection to a local repository
connection <- dbConnect(drv,
  "jdbc:lingual:local;catalog=~/src/concur/lingual/lingual-examples/
  tables;schema=EMPLOYEES")

# query the repository
df <- dbGetQuery(connection,
```

```
    "SELECT * FROM EMPLOYEES.EMPLOYEES WHERE FIRST_NAME = 'Gina'")
head(df)

# use R functions to summarize and visualize part of the data
df$hire_age <- as.integer(as.Date(df$HIRE_DATE) - as.Date(df$BIRTH_DATE)) / 365.25
summary(df$hire_age)

# uncomment next line the first time
#install.packages("ggplot2")
library(ggplot2)

m <- ggplot(df, aes(x=hire_age))
m <- m + ggtitle("Age at hire, people named Gina")
m + geom_histogram(binwidth=1, aes(y=..density.., fill=..count..)) + geom_density()
```

That R script first sets up a JDBC connection in Lingual. Then it runs the same query we used in the SQL command shell to list records for employees named Gina. Next, the script calculates age (in years) at time of hire for employees in the SQL result set. Then it calculates summary statistics and visualizes the age distribution, shown in Figure 6-5:

```
> summary(df$hire_age)
   Min. 1st Qu.  Median    Mean 3rd Qu.    Max.
  20.86   27.89   31.70   31.61   35.01   43.92
```

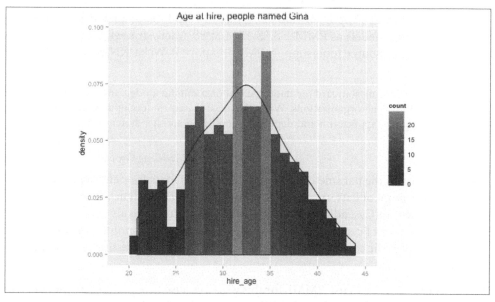

Figure 6-5. R data visualization

This shows how a very large data set could be queried to produce a sample, then analyzed —all based on R, JDBC, and SQL. Under the hood, Cascading and Apache Hadoop are doing the heavy lifting to run those queries at scale. Meanwhile, the users, analysts, and data scientists work with familiar tools and languages. That's a subtle yet powerful capability of Lingual.

Books Related to Lingual

For more information about ANSI SQL issues related to Lingual, check out these books:

- *Data Quality: The Accuracy Dimension* by Jack Olson (Morgan Kaufmann)
- *Mondrian in Action: Open source business analytics* by William Back, Nicholas Goodman, and Julian Hyde (Manning)

Pattern, a DSL for Predictive Model Markup Language

Pattern is an extension to Cascading that translates Predictive Model Markup Language (PMML) (*http://bit.ly/17TPl0z*) into Cascading apps. This open source project is a collaboration between developers at Cascading and other firms, to get coverage for several popular machine learning algorithms.

PMML is an established XML standard, since 1997, developed by a consortium called Data Modeling Group (*http://www.dmg.org/*). Many vendors for analytics frameworks support exporting models as PMML: SAS, IBM SPSS, Microstrategy, Oracle, etc. Also, many popular open source tools support PMML export: R, Weka, KNIME, RapidMiner, etc.

> PMML is the leading standard for statistical and data mining models and supported by over 20 vendors and organizations. With PMML, it is easy to develop a model on one system using one application and deploy the model on another system using another application.
>
> — Data Modeling Group

The XML captures the parameters of a model, plus metadata for defining it as a workflow. That's the point of Pattern: develop models on popular analytics frameworks, then deploy them within Cascading workflows. Benefits include greatly reduced development costs and fewer licensing issues at scale; leveraging the economics of Apache Hadoop clusters, plus the core competencies of analytics staff, plus existing IP in predictive models.

Organizations also like to use PMML for this work because several different models can be trained, and then the resulting PMML gets tagged and archived in version control. Experiments can be evaluated with A/B testing (*http://bit.ly/1aCWKS0*), multi-armed bandit (*http://bit.ly/16OOObE*), etc.; however, the source code does not have to change as the models evolve.

Initially, the focus of the Pattern project was entirely on *model scoring*:

1. Create a predictive model in an analytics framework.
2. Export the model as PMML.
3. Use Pattern to translate the PMML description into a parallelized algorithm, as a Cascading subassembly.
4. Run the model in parallel at scale on a Hadoop cluster.

More recently the project has begun work on *model creation*, where models get trained at scale using Hadoop clusters and saved as PMML. Training at scale can leverage other libraries based on Cascading, such as the Matrix API (*http://bit.ly/10zKtbs*) for Scalding. Then the model can be run at scale using the model scoring features.

Of course there are many commercial analytics frameworks used for predictive modeling. Popular tools include SAS, SAP's Hana, Oracle's Exalytics (*http://bit.ly/1aCWPoV*), Microstrategy, Microsoft SQL Server, Teradata, plus a variety of offerings from IBM such as SPSS. What these products all share is that they are expensive to license for large-scale apps.

There are Java translators for SAS such as Carolina (*http://www.dullesopen.com/*). Enterprise organizations typically look to migrate analytics workloads off of licensed frameworks and onto Hadoop clusters because of the potential for enormous cost savings. However, that migration implies the cost of rewriting and validating models in Java, Hive, Pig, etc.

In terms of Hadoop specifically, there are very good machine learning libraries available —such as Apache Mahout (*http://mahout.apache.org/*) or the Mallet toolkit (*http://mallet.cs.umass.edu/*) from UMass. However, these are tightly coupled to Apache Hadoop. They are not designed to integrate with other data frameworks and topologies, let alone leverage the Cascading flow planner.

Pattern implements large-scale, distributed algorithms in the context of Cascading as a pattern language:

- In contrast with R, it emphasizes test-driven development (TDD) at scale, with more standardized failure modes.
- In contrast with SAS, it is open sourced under an Apache ASL 2.0 license, and its algorithms run efficiently in parallel on large-scale clusters.
- In contrast with Mahout, it implements predictive models that can leverage resources beyond Hadoop while complying with best practices for Enterprise IT.

Getting Started with Pattern

Connect to a directory on your computer where you have a few gigabytes of available disk space, and then clone the source code repo from GitHub:

```
$ git clone git://github.com/Cascading/pattern.git
```

Once that completes, connect into the *pattern/pattern-examples* directory.

To verify that these steps completed correctly, let's build Pattern and run its unit tests:

```
$ gradle --info --stacktrace clean test
```

The last few lines of the console log for these unit tests should look like this:

```
Running test: test testMain(pattern.model.KMeansTest)
Running test: test testMain(pattern.model.RandomForestTest)
Gradle Worker 1 finished executing tests.
Process 'Gradle Worker 1' finished with exit value 0 (state: SUCCEEDED)

BUILD SUCCESSFUL

Total time: 13.472 secs
```

Next, we use Gradle to build the Cascading app based on Pattern that will run our PMML model. That should produce the *build/libs/pattern-examples-*.jar* JAR file. The version number within that changes.

```
$ gradle clean jar
```

A log of running this is captured in a GitHub gist (*https://gist.github.com/4588568*), and your results should be similar.

Predefined App for PMML

Pattern comes with a predefined app, which you can use to run PMML models at scale without having to write any code. A conceptual flow diagram for this app is shown in Figure 6-6, based on the Java source in the *src/main/java/pattern/pmml/Main.java* file.

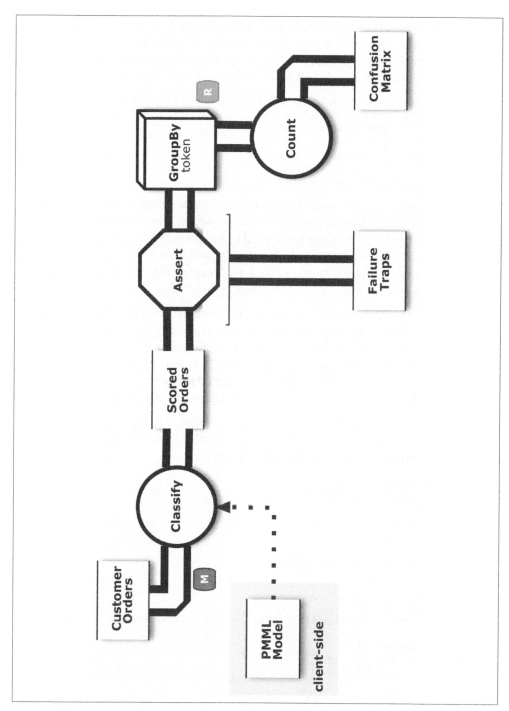

Figure 6-6. Conceptual flow diagram for predefined PMML use

Let's create a model in R, then export it as PMML, and run that model on Hadoop. The following example uses a well-known public domain data set called Iris (*http://en.wiki pedia.org/wiki/Iris_flower_data_set*), which is based on a 1936 botanical study of three species of Iris flower. Look in *data/iris.rf.tsv* for an example of this data:

```
sepal_length sepal_width petal_length petal_width species predict
5.1 3.5 1.4 0.2 setosa   setosa
4.9 3.0 1.4 0.2 setosa   setosa
5.6 2.5 3.9 1.1 versicolor   versicolor
5.9 3.2 4.8 1.8 versicolor   virginica
6.3 3.3 6.0 2.5 virginica   virginica
4.9 2.5 4.5 1.7 virginica   versicolor
```

Next, we'll create a predictive model using a machine learning algorithm called Random Forest (RF) (*http://en.wikipedia.org/wiki/Random_forest*). Random Forest is an ensemble learning method based on using a statistical technique called "bagging" with decision trees. The general idea is that one decision tree is probably never enough to capture the possible variations in a large data set. Instead, we create a collection of decision trees to help explain the various edge cases while avoiding overfitting.

In this example, the RF model uses flower measurements such as petal length to predict the iris species. The Iris data set is particularly interesting in statistics because it is provably impossible to predict all the edge cases correctly using simple linear regression methods. That presents an excellent use case for RF. The algorithm gets used widely for this reason in domains that have lots of important edge cases: for example, in finance for anti-fraud detection, and in astrophysics for detecting cosmological anomalies.

Take a look at the source code in *examples/r/pmml_models.R*, in particular the section that handles RF modeling. Here is an R script for just that model, based on the Random Forest implementation in R (*http://bit.ly/12mf5L0*):

```
install.packages("pmml")
install.packages("randomForest")
library(pmml)
library(randomForest)
require(graphics)

## split data into test and train sets
data(iris)
iris_full <- iris
colnames(iris_full) <-
  c("sepal_length", "sepal_width", "petal_length", "petal_width", "species")

idx <- sample(150, 100)
iris_train <- iris_full[idx,]
iris_test <- iris_full[-idx,]

## train a Random Forest model
f <- as.formula("as.factor(species) ~ .")
fit <- randomForest(f, data=iris_train, proximity=TRUE, ntree=50)
```

```
## report the measures of model fitness
print(fit$importance)
print(fit)
print(table(iris_test$species, predict(fit, iris_test, type="class")))

## visualize results
plot(fit, log="y", main="Random Forest")
varImpPlot(fit)
MDSplot(fit, iris_full$species)

## export PMML + test data
out <- iris_full
out$predict <- predict(fit, out, type="class")

dat_folder <- './data'
tsv <- paste(dat_folder, "iris.rf.tsv", sep="/")
write.table(out, file=tsv, quote=FALSE, sep="\t", row.names=FALSE)
saveXML(pmml(fit), file=paste(dat_folder, "iris.rf.xml", sep="/"))
```

The R script loads the required packages, along with the Iris data set. It splits the data set into two parts: iris_train and iris_test. Then it trains a Random Forest model using the iris_train part, using the petal and sepal measures to predict species.

The results of this model creation get evaluated and visualized in a few different ways. First we have a few printed reports about the fitness of the model. One well-known aspect of the Iris data set is that the "setosa" species is relatively easy to predict, whereas the other two species have overlap, which confuses predictive models. We see that in the results, but overall there is an estimated 5% error rate:

```
        OOB estimate of  error rate: 5%
Confusion matrix:
           setosa versicolor virginica class.error
setosa         32          0         0  0.00000000
versicolor      0         26         2  0.07142857
virginica       0          3        37  0.07500000
```

The chart in Figure 6-7 shows error rate versus the number of trees. One of the parameters for training an RF model is to select the number of trees in the forest. As that parameter approaches 50 trees, decrease in error levels out.

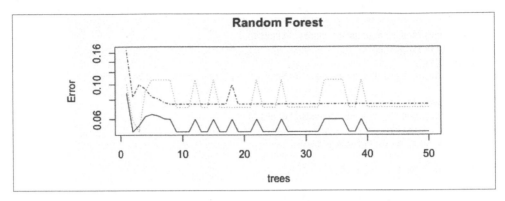

Figure 6-7. RF model—error versus trees

The chart in Figure 6-8 shows the mean decrease in the Gini ratio (*http://en.wikipe dia.org/wiki/Gini_coefficient*) for each independent variable used in the model. In this case, petal_width is the best predictor.

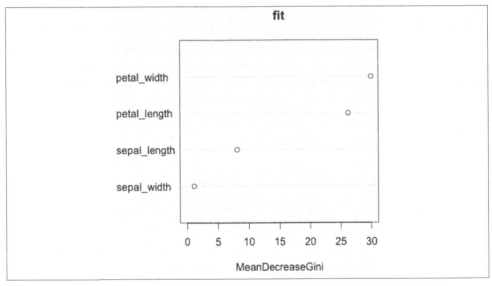

Figure 6-8. RF model—mean decrease Gini

The chart in Figure 6-9 shows a multidimensional scaling (MDS) plot for the proximity matrix.

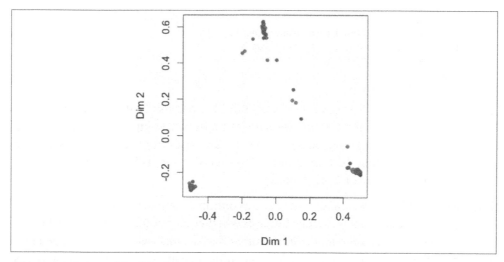

Figure 6-9. RF model—MDS proximity matrix

The plot shows the principal components of the distance matrix—points that are close together represent data points that are similar to each other. This is one way of showing outliers that haven't been handled well by the model. Again, we know that the "setosa" species clusters tightly, whereas "versicolor" and "virginica" tend to overlap.

The remainder of the R script writes the data with a column added to represent the expected results from the model for us to use in regression testing. Then it writes the PMML file to capture the model. Take a look at the resulting XML definitions in the *data/iris.rf.xml* file:

```
<MiningModel
  modelName="randomForest_Model"
  functionName="classification"
  >
<MiningSchema>
  <MiningField name="species" usageType="predicted"/>
  <MiningField name="sepal_length" usageType="active"/>
  <MiningField name="sepal_width" usageType="active"/>
  <MiningField name="petal_length" usageType="active"/>
  <MiningField name="petal_width" usageType="active"/>
</MiningSchema>
...
```

Now that we have a PMML model, let's use Pattern to run it. We'll run a regression test to confirm that the results predicted on Hadoop match those predicted in R as a baseline. Then we'll calculate a confusion matrix (*http://bit.ly/123vgwN*) to evaluate the error rates in the model. Again, a log of a successful run is given in a GitHub gist (*https://gist.github.com/4588568*) to compare:

```
$ rm -rf out
$ hadoop jar build/libs/pattern-examples-*.jar \
  data/iris.rf.tsv out/classify out/trap \
  --pmml data/iris.rf.xml \
  --assert \
  --measure out/measure
```

First, we clear the *out* directory used for output files, because Hadoop will check for it and fail the app rather than overwrite data. We specify the input data source `data/iris.rf.tsv`, output data sink `out/classify/*`, and also `out/trap` as a trap sink. The latter is used for catching bad input data. The `--pmml data/iris.rf.xml` command-line argument specifies our PMML model.

Note that we add `--assert` and `--measure` as optional command-line arguments. For each tuple in the data, a stream assertion tests whether the `predicted` field matches the `score` field generated by the model in R. Tuples that fail that assertion get trapped into `out/trap/part*` for inspection later. Also, a confusion matrix gets written to `out/measure/part*` output, based on `species` as the predicted field. We measure the performance of the predictive model, counting how many false positives or false negatives result.

The output shows that model had a 100% success rate for the regression test. If there had been any difference between the Pattern results and the R results, Cascading stream assertions would have rejected those output tuples and shown exceptions in the console log:

```
$ head out/classify/part-00000
sepal_length sepal_width   petal_length    petal_width species predict score
5.1 3.5 1.4 0.2 setosa   setosa   setosa
4.9 3   1.4 0.2 setosa   setosa   setosa
4.7 3.2 1.3 0.2 setosa   setosa   setosa
4.6 3.1 1.5 0.2 setosa   setosa   setosa
5   3.6 1.4 0.2 setosa   setosa   setosa
5.4 3.9 1.7 0.4 setosa   setosa   setosa
4.6 3.4 1.4 0.3 setosa   setosa   setosa
5   3.4 1.5 0.2 setosa   setosa   setosa
4.4 2.9 1.4 0.2 setosa   setosa   setosa
$
$ head out/measure/part-00000
species     score       count
setosa      setosa      50
versicolor  versicolor  48
versicolor  virginica   2
virginica   versicolor  1
virginica   virginica   49
```

As expected, there is approximately 5% error overall. The `setosa` species gets predicted correctly, whereas the other two species have some overlap.

Integrating Pattern into Cascading Apps

Let's take a look at how to incorporate Pattern into a Cascading app. This requires only two additional lines of source code. The following shows a minimal Cascading app that uses Pattern, starting with the set up for a `Main.java` class:

```java
public class Main {
  public static void main( String[] args ) {
    String pmmlPath = args[ 0 ];
    String inputPath = args[ 1 ];
    String classifyPath = args[ 2 ];
    String trapPath = args[ 3 ];

    Properties properties = new Properties();
    AppProps.setApplicationJarClass( properties, Main.class );
    HadoopFlowConnector flowConnector =
      new HadoopFlowConnector( properties );
```

Next, we define three Cascading taps for input, output, and trap:

```java
Tap inputTap =
  new Hfs( new TextDelimited( true, "\t" ), inputPath );
Tap classifyTap =
  new Hfs( new TextDelimited( true, "\t" ), classifyPath );
Tap trapTap =
  new Hfs( new TextDelimited( true, "\t" ), trapPath );
```

Then we use the `PMMLPlanner` in Pattern to parse the predictive model and build a `SubAssembly`. The PMML file is referenced as a command-line argument called `pmmlPath` in the following code:

```java
PMMLPlanner pmmlPlanner = new PMMLPlanner()
  .setPMMLInput( new File( pmmlPath ) )
  .retainOnlyActiveIncomingFields()
  .setDefaultPredictedField( new Fields( "predict", Double.class ) );

flowDef.addAssemblyPlanner( pmmlPlanner );
```

Those are the only lines required for Pattern, other than its package import. In Cascalog or Scalding, this would require even less code.

Finally, we call the flow planner to create a physical plan and then submit the job to Hadoop:

```java
Flow classifyFlow = flowConnector.connect( flowDef );
classifyFlow.writeDOT( "dot/classify.dot" );
classifyFlow.complete();
```

Customer Experiments

There has been much interest in leveraging Pattern, Cascading, and Apache Hadoop to run customer experiments at scale. The idea is to generate multiple variants of a predictive model, each exported as PMML. Then run these models on a Hadoop cluster with large-scale customer data. Finally, use analysis of the confusion matrix results to measure the relative lift among models.

To show an example, first we need some data to use for an experiment. The code on GitHub includes a Python script to generate sample data sets. Take a look at the *examples/py/gen_orders.py* file. That script can be used to create a relatively large data set (e.g., terabyte scale) for training and evaluating the PMML models on a Hadoop cluster:

```python
#!/usr/bin/env python
# encoding: utf-8
import random
import sys
import uuid

CUSTOMER_SEGMENTS = (
    [0.2, ["0", random.gauss, 0.25, 0.75, "%0.2f"]],
    [0.8, ["0", random.gauss, 1.5, 0.25, "%0.2f"]],
    [0.9, ["1", random.gauss, 0.6, 0.2, "%0.2f"]],
    [1.0, ["1", random.gauss, 0.75, 0.2, "%0.2f"]]
)

def gen_row (segments, num_col):
    coin_flip = random.random()

    for prob, rand_var in segments:
        if coin_flip <= prob:
            (label, dist, mean, sigma, f) = rand_var
            order_id = str(uuid.uuid1()).split("-")[0]
            d = dist(mean, sigma)
            m = map(lambda x: f % d, range(0, num_col))
            return [label] + m + [order_id]

if __name__ == '__main__':
    num_row = int(sys.argv[1])
    num_col = int(sys.argv[2])

    m = map(lambda x: "v" + str(x), range(0, num_col))
    print "\t".join(["label"] + m + ["order_id"])

    for i in range(0, num_row):
        print "\t".join(gen_row(CUSTOMER_SEGMENTS, num_col))
```

We run this script with command-line arguments to specify the number of rows and columns. For example, the following creates 1,000 rows with 50 independent variables each:

```
./examples/py/gen_orders.py 50 1000
```

A small example is given in the *data/sample.tsv* file:

```
label   var0    var1    var2    order_id        predict
1       0       1       0       6f8e1014        1
0       0       0       1       6f8ea22e        0
1       0       1       0       6f8ea435        1
...
```

Next, we use this data to create a model based on Random Forest—like in the earlier example. The `label` dependent variable gets predicted based on `var0`, `var1`, and `var2` as independent variables:

```
## train a Random Forest model
## example: http://mkseo.pe.kr/stats/?p=220

f <- as.formula("as.factor(label) ~ var0 + var1 + var2")
fit <- randomForest(f, data=data, proximity=TRUE, ntree=25)
print(fit)
saveXML(pmml(fit), file-"sample.rf.xml")
```

Output from R shows an estimated 14% error rate for this model:

```
        OOB estimate of  error rate: 14%
Confusion matrix:
     0   1 class.error
0 69  16   0.1882353
1 12 103   0.1043478
```

Next, we use the same data to train a model based on a different algorithm, Logistic Regression (*http://en.wikipedia.org/wiki/Logistic_regression*). To help illustrate experiment results later, one of the independent variables `var1` is omitted from the model:

```
## train a Logistic Regression model (special case of GLM)
## example: http://www.stat.cmu.edu/~cshalizi/490/clustering/clustering01.r

f <- as.formula("as.factor(label) ~ var0 + var2")
fit <- glm(f, family=binomial, data=data)
print(summary(fit))
saveXML(pmml(fit), file="sample.lr.xml")
```

Now we can use the predefined app in Pattern to run both models and collect their confusion matrix results:

```
$ rm -rf out
$ hadoop jar build/libs/pattern-examples-*.jar \
  data/sample.tsv out/classify.rf out/trap \
  --pmml sample.rf.xml --measure out/measure
$ mv out/classify.rf .
```

```
$ rm -rf out
$ hadoop jar build/libs/pattern-examples-*.jar \
  data/sample.tsv out/classify.lr out/trap \
  --pmml sample.lr.xml --measure out/measure
$ mv out/classify.lr .
```

It would be reasonably simple to build a Cascading app to do the comparisons between models, i.e., a framework for customer experiments. That would be especially useful if there were a large number of models to compare. In this case, we can compare results using a spreadsheet as shown in Figure 6-10.

		logistic regression						random forest		
		score		total				score		total
		0	1					0	1	
label	0	41	44	85		label	0	73	12	85
	1	6	109	115			1	13	102	115
		0.482	0.518					0.859	0.141	
		0.052	0.948					0.113	0.887	
		TN	FP					TN	FP	
		FN	TP					FN	TP	

Figure 6-10. Customer experiment

The model based on Logistic Regression has a lower rate (5% versus 11%) for false negatives (FN). However, that model has a much higher rate (52% versus 14%) for false positives (FP).

Let's put this into terms that decision makers use in business to determine which model is better. For example, in the case of an anti-fraud classifier used in ecommerce, we can assign a cost function to select a winner of the experiment. On one hand, a higher rate of false negatives implies that more fraudulent orders fail to get flagged for review. Ultimately that results in a higher rate of *chargeback* fines from the bank, and punitive actions by the credit card processor if that rate goes too high for too long. So the FN rate is proportional to chargeback risk in ecommerce. On the other hand, a higher rate of false positives implies that more legitimate orders get flagged for review. Ultimately that results in more complaints from actual customers, and higher costs for customer support. So the FP rate is proportional to support costs in ecommerce.

Evaluating this experiment, the Logistic Regression model—which had a variable omitted to exaggerate the comparison—resulted in approximately half the FN rate, compared with the Random Forest model. However, it also resulted in quadrupled costs for customer support. A decision maker can use those cost trade-offs to select the appropriate model for the business needs.

One important issue to keep in mind about analytics frameworks is that it tends to be expensive or impossible to run models at scale. Running multiple models, such as for extensive customer experiments, compounds that problem. By using Pattern, Cascading, and Apache Hadoop, organizations can now scale their experiments, adding more science to the practice of data-driven business.

Technology Roadmap for Pattern

As of version 4.01, PMML supports quite a number of different families of predictive models:

Association Rules
   `AssociationModel` element

Cluster Models
   `ClusteringModel` element

Decision Trees
   `TreeModel` element

Naïve Bayes Classifiers
   `NaiveBayesModel` element

Neural Networks
   `NeuralNetwork` element

Regression
   `RegressionModel` and `GeneralRegressionModel` elements

Rule Sets
   `RuleSetModel` element

Sequences
   `SequenceModel` element

Support Vector Machines
   `SupportVectorMachineModel` element

Text Analytics
   `TextModel` element

Time Series
   `TimeSeriesModel` element

The structure of a PMML document is quite interesting in the context of Cascading. The input variables are defined in a metadata section. It's possible to define some forms of preprocessing and post-processing. Models can be combined into *ensembles*, such as how Random Forest is an ensemble of decision trees. That has become a powerful strategy in commercial applications of machine learning. Moreover, PMML combines these definitions into an expression of business process for a complex data workflow. Overall, that maps to Cascading quite closely—input and output variables in PMML correspond to tuple flows, with the Cascading flow planners providing parallelization for predictive model algorithms on Hadoop clusters.

Currently there are several companies collaborating on the Pattern project. Besides the Random Forest and Logistic Regression algorithms, other PMML implementations include the following:

- Linear Regression (*http://en.wikipedia.org/wiki/Linear_regression*)
- K-Means Clustering (*http://en.wikipedia.org/wiki/K-means_clustering*)
- Hierarchical Clustering (*http://en.wikipedia.org/wiki/Hierarchical_clustering*)
- Support Vector Machines (*http://en.wikipedia.org/wiki/Support_vector_machine*)

Linear regression is probably the most common form of predictive model, such as in Microsoft Excel spreadsheets. K-means is widely used for customer segmentation, document search, and other kinds of predictive models.

Other good PMML resources include the following:

- Data Mining Group (*http://www.dmg.org/*)—XML standards and supported vendors
- Zementis PMML validator (*http://www.zementis.com/pmml_tools.htm*)
- PMML group on LinkedIn (*http://linkd.in/1b7Xrl0*)
- "Representing predictive solutions in PMML" (*http://ibm.co/12H1Z9V*) by Alex Guazzelli

Books Related to Pattern

For more information about PMML and predictive models in general, check out these books:

- *PMML in Action* by Alex Guazzelli, Wen-Ching Lin, and Tridivesh Jena (CreateSpace)
- *Mining of Massive Datasets* by Anand Rajaraman and Jeffrey Ullman (Cambridge University Press)

## CHAPTER 7

The Workflow Abstraction

Key Insights

Thus far, we have looked at several examples of how to use Cascading. Now let's step back a bit and take a look at some of the theory at its foundation.

The author of Cascading, Chris Wensel, was working at a large firm known well for many data products. Wensel was evaluating the Nutch project, which included Lucene and subsequently Hadoop—he was evaluating how to leverage these open source technologies for Big Data within an Enterprise environment. His takeaway was that it would be difficult to find enough Java developers who could write complex Enterprise apps directly in MapReduce.

An obvious response would have been to build some kind of abstraction layer atop Hadoop. Many different variations of this have been developed over the years, and that approach dates back to the many "fourth-generation languages" (4GL) starting in the 1970s. However, another takeaway Wensel had from the early days of Apache Hadoop use was that abstraction layers built by and for the early adopters typically would not pass the "bench test" for Enterprise. The operational complexity of large-scale apps and the need to leverage many existing software engineering practices would be difficult if not impossible to manage through a 4GL-styled abstraction layer.

A key insight into this problem was that MapReduce is based on the functional programming paradigm. In the original MapReduce paper (*http://research.google.com/ archive/mapreduce.html*) by Jeffrey Dean and Sanjay Ghemawat at Google, the authors made clear that a functional programming model allowed for the following:

- Apps to be automatically parallelized on large clusters of commodity hardware
- Programmers who didn't have experience with parallel/distributed processing to leverage large clusters
- Data frameworks "to use re-execution as the primary mechanism for fault tolerance"

The general pattern of parallelism achieved through a MapReduce framework traces back to what the AI community was doing in LISP in the 1970s and 1980s at MIT, Stanford, CMU, etc. Also, most of the nontrivial Hadoop apps are data pipelines—which are functional in essence.

The innovation of Cascading, in late 2007, was to introduce a Java API for functional programming with large-scale data workflows. As we've seen thus far, this approach allowed for a plumbing metaphor based on functional programming, which was very close to the use cases for Hadoop but abstracted a much higher level than writing Map-Reduce code directly. At the same time, this approach leveraged the JVM and Java-based tools without any need to create or support new languages. Programmers who had Java expertise could leverage the economics of Hadoop clusters yet still use their familiar tools.

In doing this, Cascading resolved many issues related to Hadoop use in Enterprise environments. Notably, it did the following:

- Eased the "staffing bottleneck," because Java developers could work with familiar tools and processes
- Improved means for system integration, because Hadoop is rarely ever used in isolation, and the abstraction integrated other frameworks
- Reduced the operational complexity of large-scale apps by keeping apps defined as single JAR files
- Allowed for TDD and other software engineering practices at scale

A subtle point about the design of Cascading is that it created a foundation for building other abstraction layers in JVM-based functional programming languages. Codd had suggested the use of DSLs for manipulating the relational model as early as 1969. The proof is in the pudding, because Twitter, Etsy, eBay, The Climate Corporation, uSwitch, Nokia, LinkedIn, etc., have invested considerable engineering resources into developing and extending open source projects—Cascalog, Scalding, PyCascading, Cascading.JRuby, etc.—all based on functional programming. In turn they have built out their revenue apps, along with many other firms, based on those projects.

There are a few important theoretical aspects embodied by these data workflow abstractions based on Cascading. Those elements of theory can best be explained as layers in the process of structuring data:

- Pattern language
- Literate programming
- Separation of concerns
- Functional relational paradigm

Pattern Language

Formally speaking, Cascading represents a pattern language. The notion of a pattern language is that the syntax of the language constrains what can be expressed to help ensure best practices. Stated in another way, a pattern language conveys expertise. For example, consider how a child builds a tower out of Lego blocks. The blocks snap together in predictable ways, allowing for complex structures that are reasonably sturdy. When the blocks are not snapped together properly, those structures tend to fall over. Lego blocks therefore provide a way of conveying expertise about building toy structures.

Use of pattern language came from architecture, based on work by Christopher Alexander on the "Oregon Experiment." Kent Beck and Ward Cunningham subsequently used it to describe software design patterns, popularized by the "Gang of Four"—Erich Gamma, Richard Helm, Ralph Johnson, and John Vlissides—for object-oriented programming. Abstract Factory, Model-View-Controller (MVC), and Facade are examples of well-known software design patterns.

Cascading uses pattern language to ensure best practices specifically for robust, parallel data workflows at scale. We see the pattern syntax enforced in several ways. For example, flows must have at least one source and at least one tail sink defined. For another example, aggregator functions such as Count must be used in an Every; in other words, that work gets performed in a reduce task.

Another benefit of pattern language in Cascading is that it promotes code reuse. Rather, it reduces the need for writing custom operations because much of the needed business process can be defined by combing existing components. In a larger context, this is related to the use of patterns in enterprise application integration (EAI).

Literate Programming

The philosophy of literate programming was originated by Donald Knuth. A reasonable summary would be to say that instead of writing documentation about programs, write documents that embed programs. We see this practice quite directly in terms of the flow diagrams used in Cascading. A flow diagram is also a common expression of the business process in a Cascading app, even though different portions of that process may have been specified in Java, Clojure, Scala, Python, Ruby, ANSI SQL, PMML, etc. A flow diagram is the literal representation for the query that will run in parallel on a cluster.

> Instead of imagining that our main task is to instruct a computer what to do, let us concentrate rather on explaining to human beings what we want a computer to do.
>
> — Literate Programming
> *Donald Knuth (1992)*

When a Cascading app runs, it creates a flow diagram that can optionally be written to a DOT file. Flow diagrams provide intuitive, visual representations for apps, which are great for cross-team collaboration. Several good examples exist, but one is the phenomenon of different developers troubleshooting a Cascading app together over the `cascading-users` email forum. Expert developers generally ask a novice to provide a flow diagram first, often before asking to see source code. For instance, a flow diagram for "Example 2: The Ubiquitous Word Count" is provided in Figure 7-1.

Another good example is found in Scalding apps, which have a nearly 1:1 correspondence between function calls and the elements in their flow diagrams. This demonstrates excellent efficiency for language elision and literate representation. The benefit, in engineering terms, is that this property helps make the complex logic embodied in a Scalding app relatively simple to understand.

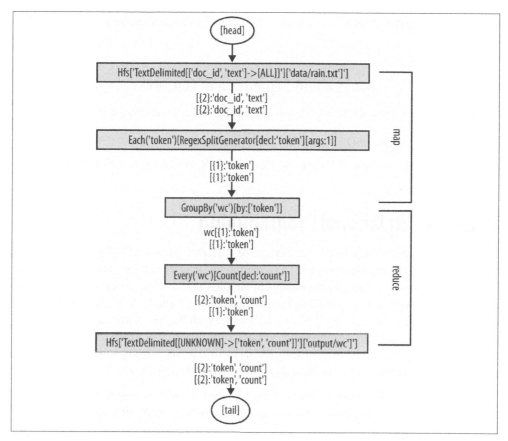

Figure 7-1. Annotated flow diagram for "Example 2: The Ubiquitous Word Count"

Separation of Concerns

Based on the philosophy of literate programming, Cascading workflows emphasize the statement of business processes. This recalls a sense of business process management (BPM) for Enterprise apps. In other words, think of BPM/BPEL for Big Data as a means for workflow orchestration—in this case Cascading provides a kind of middleware. It creates a separation of concerns between the business process required for an app and its implementation details, such as Hadoop jobs, data serialization protocols, etc.

By virtue of the pattern language, the flow planners in Cascading have guarantees that they will be able to translate business processes into efficient, parallel code at scale. That is a kind of "one-two punch" in Cascading, leveraging computer science theory in different layers.

Books about Separation of Concerns

For more information about literate programming and separation of concerns:

- *Literate Programming* by Donald Knuth (Stanford)
- *Elements Of Functional Programming* by Chris Reade (Addison-Wesley)

Functional Relational Programming

Cascalog developers describe the separation of concerns between business process and implementation (parallelization, etc.) as a principle: "specify what you require, not how it must be achieved." That's an important principle because in practice, quite arguably, developing Enterprise data workflows is an inherently complex matter. The frameworks for distributed systems such as Hadoop, HBase, Cassandra, Memcached, etc. introduce lots of complexity into the engineering process. Typical kinds of problems being solved, often leveraging machine learning algorithms to find a proverbial needle in a haystack within large data sets, also introduce significant complexity into apps.

The author of Cascalog, Nathan Marz, noted a general problem about Big Data frameworks: that the tools being used to solve a given problem can sometimes introduce more complexity than the problem itself. We call this phenomenon accidental complexity (*http://en.wikipedia.org/wiki/Accidental_complexity*), and it represents an important anti-pattern in computer science.

> A lot of people talk about how wonderfully expressive Clojure is. However, expressiveness is not the goal of Clojure. Clojure aims to minimize accidental complexity, and its expressiveness is a means to that end.
>
> — Nathan Marz
> *Twitter (2011)*

There are limits to how much complexity people can understand at any given point, limits to how well we can understand the systems on which we rely. Some approaches to software design amplify that problem. For example, reading 50,000 lines of COBOL is not particularly simple. SQL and Java are notorious for encouraging the development of large, complicated apps. So it makes sense to prevent artifacts in our programming languages from making Enterprise data workflows even more complex.

Referring back to the original 1969 paper about the relational model (*http://en.wikipedia.org/wiki/Relational_model*), Edgar Codd focused on the process of structuring data as a mechanism for maintaining data integrity and consistency of state, while providing

---

a separation of concerns regarding data storage and representation underneath. This description is quite apt for the workflow abstraction in Cascading. Codd's first public paper about the relational model is archived in the ACM Digital Library (*http://dl.acm.org/citation.cfm?id=362685*).

More recently, in the highly influential 2006 paper "Out of the Tar Pit," Ben Moseley and Peter Marks proposed *functional relational programming* (FRP) as a combination of three major programming paradigms: functional, relational, and logical. FRP is proposed as an alternative to object-oriented programming (OOP) (*http://bit.ly/14qVInc*), with the intent to minimize the accidental complexity introduced into apps. For more information about FRP, see the following:

- FRP paper (*http://citeseerx.ist.psu.edu/viewdoc/summary?doi=10.1.1.93.8928*)
- FRP presentation (*http://www.scribd.com/doc/3566845/FRP-Presentation-Web*)
- FRP email list (*https://groups.google.com/forum/#!forum/frp-discuss*)

> When it comes to accidental and essential complexity we firmly believe that the former exists and that the goal of software engineering must be both to eliminate as much of it as possible, and to assist with the latter.
>
> — Moseley and Marks
> *"Out of the Tar Pit" (2006)*

Moseley and Marks attempted to categorize the different kinds of complexity encountered in software engineering, and analyzed the dimensions of *state*, *code volume*, and explicit (imperative) concern with the flow of *control* through a system. They noted that "complexity breeds complexity" in the absence of language-enforced guarantees—in other words, it creates positive feedback loops in software practice. They pointed out that complexity that derives from state is one of the biggest hurdles for making code testable. Their paper also considered the origins of the relational model, going back to Codd:

> In FRP all essential state takes the form of relations, and the essential logic is expressed using relational algebra extended with (pure) user-defined functions.
>
> — Moseley and Marks
> *"Out of the Tar Pit" (2006)*

In other words, if we can cut out the unnecessary state represented in an app and focus on the essential state (relations) we can eliminate much of the accidental complexity. Cascading embodies much of that philosophy, putting FRP into the practice of building Enterprise data workflows. Cascading and FRP have several important aspects of computer science theory in common:

- A workflow is represented as a static DAG.
- Only the root nodes of the DAG are mutable, i.e., the source taps.

- All the nodes in the DAG are relations, e.g., pipes and operations.
- The practice of programming this DAG separates logical aspects from control aspects.

Moseley and Marks also point toward a management approach indicated by FRP. For example, an organization could focus one team on minimizing the accidental aspects of a system. Other teams could then focus on the essential aspects, providing the infrastructure and the requirements for interfacing with other systems. Roughly speaking, that corresponds respectively to the roles of developer, data scientist, ops, etc.; however, the objectives of those teams become clarified through FRP. It also fits well with what is shown in Figure 6-3 for cross-team functional integration based on Cascading.

Enterprise vs. Start-Ups

In summary, there are several theoretical aspects of the workflow abstraction. These get leveraged in Cascading and the DSLs to help minimize the complexity of the engineering process, and the complexity of understanding systems.

Generally speaking, in terms of Enterprise data workflows, there are two avenues to the party—scale versus complexity—a contrast that is seen quite starkly in use case analysis of Cascading deployments.

On one hand, there are Enterprise firms where people must contend with complexity at scale all day, every day. Incumbents in the Enterprise space make very large investments in their back office infrastructure and practices—generally using Java, ANSI SQL, SAS, etc., and have a large staff trained in those systems and processes. While the incumbents typically face considerable challenges in trying to be innovative, they are faced with multiple priorities for migrating workflows onto Apache Hadoop. One priority is based on economics: scaling out a machine learning app on a Hadoop cluster implies much less in licensing costs than running the app in SAS. Another priority is risk management: being able to scale efficiently and rapidly, when the business requires it. Meanwhile, a big part of the challenge is to leverage existing staff and integrate infrastructure without disrupting established processes. The workflow abstraction in Cascading addresses those issues directly.

On the other hand, start-ups crave complexity and must scale to become viable. Start-ups are generally good at innovation and light on existing process. They tend to leverage sophisticated engineering practices—e.g., Cascalog and Scalding—so that they can have a relatively lean staff while positioning to compete against the Enterprise incumbents and disrupt their market share. Cascading provides the foundation for DSLs in functional programming languages that help power those ventures.

There is a transition curve plotted along the dimensions of scale, complexity, and innovation. One perspective of this is shown in Figure 7-2.

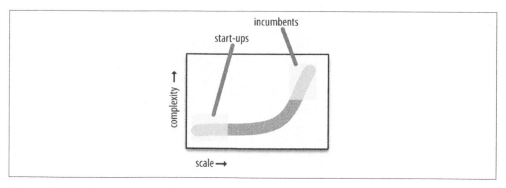

Figure 7-2. Scale versus complexity

Both the Enterprise incumbents and the start-ups are connected on that curve for any given Big Data project. Ultimately, when they succeed, they tend to meet in the middle. Dijkstra foresaw this relationship quite clearly:

> Computing's core challenge is how not to make a mess of it. If people object that any science has to meet that challenge, we should give a double rebuttal. Firstly, machines are so fast and storage capacities are so huge that we face orders of magnitude more room for confusion, the propagation and diffusion of which are easily inadvertently mechanized. Secondly, because we are dealing with artefacts, all unmastered complexity is of our own making; there is no one else to blame and so we had better learn how not to introduce the complexity in the first place.[1]
>
> — Edsger Dijkstra
> *The next fifty years*

1. *http://www.cs.utexas.edu/~EWD/transcriptions/EWD12xx/EWD1243a.html*

## CHAPTER 8

Case Study: City of Palo Alto Open Data

Why Open Data?

When people first start to work with Cascading, one frequent question is "Where can I get large data sets to use for examples?" For great sources of data sets, look toward Open Data. Many governments at the city, state, and federal levels have initiatives to make much of their data openly available. Open Data gives a community greater visibility into how its government functions. The general idea is that people within the community—entrepreneurs, students, social groups, etc.—will find novel ways to leverage that data. In turn, the results of those efforts benefit the public good.

Here are some good examples of Open Data and other publically available repositories:

- *http://explore.data.gov/*
- *http://open-data.europa.eu/open-data/*
- *http://commoncrawl.org/*
- *http://marinexplore.org/*
- *http://data.worldbank.org/*
- *http://geocommons.com/*
- *http://archive.ics.uci.edu/ml/*

City of Palo Alto

The sample app discussed in this chapter was originally developed for a graduate engineering seminar at Carnegie Mellon University. The intent was to create an example Cascading app based on the Open Data initiative by the City of Palo Alto. Many thanks for help with this project go to Dr. Stuart Evans, CMU Distinguished Service Professor;

Jonathan Reichental, CIO for the City of Palo Alto; and Diego May, CEO of Junar, the company that provided the data infrastructure for this initiative and many others.

Thinking about Palo Alto and its Open Data initiative, a few ideas come to mind. The city is generally quite a pleasant place: the weather is temperate, there are lots of parks with enormous trees, most of downtown is quite walkable, and it's not particularly crowded. On a summer day in Palo Alto, one of the last things anybody really wants is to be stuck in an office on a long phone call. Instead people walk outside and take their calls, probably heading toward a favorite espresso bar or a popular frozen yogurt shop. On a hot summer day in Palo Alto, knowing a nice route to walk in the shade would be great. There must be a smartphone app for that—but as of late 2012, there wasn't!

In this chapter, we'll build an example Cascading workflow for that smartphone app as a case study. A sample app (*https://github.com/Cascading/CoPA/wiki*) is shown in both Java and Clojure to power a mobile data API.

Imagine a mobile app that leverages the city's municipal data to personalize recommendations: "Find a shady spot on a summer day in which to walk near downtown Palo Alto. While on a long conference call. Sippin' a latte or enjoying some fro-yo." This app shows the process of structuring data as a workflow, progressing from raw sources to refine that process until we obtain the data products for that recommender. The results are personalized based on the neighborhoods where a person tends to walk.

To download source code, first connect to a directory on your computer where you have a few gigabytes of available disk space, and then use Git to clone the source code repo:

```
$ git clone git://github.com/Cascading/CoPA.git
```

Once that download completes, connect into that newly cloned directory. Source code is shown in both Cascading (Java) and Cascalog (Clojure). We'll work through the Cascalog example, and its source is located in the *src/main/clj/copa/core.clj* file.

Moving from Raw Sources to Data Products

The City of Palo Alto has its Open Data portal available online (*http://paloalto.openda ta.junar.com/*). It publishes a wide range of different data sets: budget history, census data, geographic information systems (GIS) as shown in Figure 8-1, building permits, utility consumption rates, street sweeping schedules, creek levels, etc.

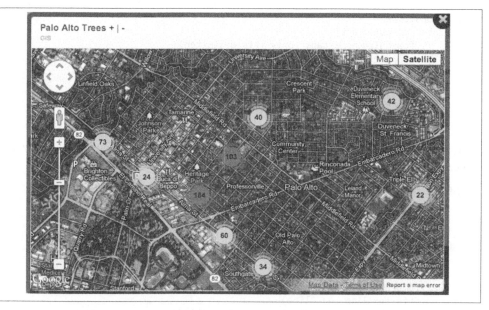

Figure 8-1. GIS data about trees in Palo Alto

For this app, we use parts of the GIS export—in particular the location data about trees and roads. Most governments track components of their infrastructure using a GIS system. ArcGIS (*http://www.esri.com/software/arcgis*) is a popular software platform for that kind of work. Palo Alto exports its GIS data, which you can download from the portal on Junar. A copy is also given in the *data/copa.csv* file.

Take a look at one of the tree records in the GIS export:

```
$ cat data/copa.csv | grep "HAWTHORNE AV 22"

"Tree: 412 site 1 at 115 HAWTHORNE AV, on HAWTHORNE AV 22 from pl",
"   Private:   -1   Tree ID:   412   Street_Name:   HAWTHORNE AV
 Situs Number:   115   Tree Site:   1   Species:   Liquidambar styraciflua
 Source:   davey tree   Protected:   Designated:   Heritage:
 Appraised Value:   Hardscape:   None   Identifier:   474
 Active Numeric:   1   Location Feature ID:   18583
 Provisional:   Install Date:   ",
"37.446001565119,-122.167713417554,0.0 ",
"Point"
```

Clearly that is an example of unstructured data. Our next step is to structure those kinds of records into tuple streams that we can use in our workflow.

Looking at the source code located in the *src/main/clj/copa/core.clj* file, the first several lines define a Clojure namespace for importing required libraries:

```
(ns copa.core
  (:use [cascalog.api]
        [cascalog.more-taps :only (hfs-delimited)]
        [date-clj])
  (:require [clojure.string :as s]
            [cascalog [ops :as c]]
            [clojure-csv.core :as csv]
            [geohash.core :as geo])
  (:gen-class))
```

Next, there are two functions that begin to parse and structure the raw data from the GIS export:

```
(def parse-csv
  "parse complex CSV format in the unclean GIS export"
  (comp first csv/parse-csv))

(defn load-gis
  "Parse GIS csv data"
  [in trap]
  (<- [?blurb ?misc ?geo ?kind]
      ((hfs-textline in) ?line)
      (parse-csv ?line :> ?blurb ?misc ?geo ?kind)
      (:trap (hfs-textline trap))))
```

The GIS data is exported in comma-separated values (CSV) format. There are missing values and other errors in the export, so we need to handle the parsing specially. The load-gis function reads each line using the hfs-textline tap, then parses those into tuples using the csv/parse-csv Clojure library. A trap collects any data lines that are not formatted properly. In this case the trapped data does not contain much information, so we simply ignore it.

One side note about process: in data science work, we typically encounter an 80/20 rule such that 80% of the time and costs go toward cleaning up the data, while 20% of the time and costs get spent on the science used to obtain actionable insights. The better tools and frameworks help to balance and reduce those costs. It's true in this app that most of the code is needed for data preparation, while the recommender portion is only a few lines. Even so, Cascalog helps make that data preparation process relatively simple. Here we invoke the principle of "Specify what you require, not how to achieve it." In just a few lines of Clojure, we state the requirement to derive four fields (blurb, misc, geo, kind) from the GIS export, and trap (discard) records that fail to follow that pattern.

Next we need to focus on structuring the tree data. Looking in the example record shown previously, the tree has several properties listed. There is a unique identifier (412), a street address (115 Hawthorne Av), a species name (Liquidambar styraciflua), etc., plus its geo coordinates. Our goal is to find a quiet shady spot in which to walk and take a cell phone call. We definitely know about the location of each tree, but what can we determine about shade? Given the tree species, we could look up average height and use

---

that as an estimator for shade. So the next step is to use a regular expression to parse the tree properties, such as address and species, from the `misc` field:

```
(defn re-seq-chunks [pattern s]
  (rest (first (re-seq pattern s))))

(def parse-tree
  "parses the special fields in the tree format"
  (partial re-seq-chunks
    #"^\s+Private\:\s+(\S+)\s+Tree ID\:\s+(\d+)\s+.*Situs
    Number\:\s+(\d+)\s+Tree Site\:\s+(\d+)\s+Species\:\s+(\S.*\S)\s+Source.*"
    ))
```

Great, now we begin to have some structured data about trees:

```
Identifier:    474
Tree ID:       412
Tree:          412 site 1 at 115 HAWTHORNE AV
Tree Site:     1
Street_Name:   HAWTHORNE AV
Situs Number: 115
Private:       -1
Species:       Liquidambar styraciflua
Source:        davey tree
Hardscape:     None
```

We can use the species name to join with a table of tree species metadata and look up average height, along with inferring other valuable data. Take a look in the *data/meta_tree.tsv* file to see the metadata about trees, which was derived from Wikipedia.org, Calflora.org, USDA.gov, etc. The species *liquidambar styraciflua*, commonly known as an American sweetgum, grows to a height that ranges between 20 and 35 meters.

The next section of code completes our definition of a data product about trees. The `geo-tree` function parses the geo coordinates: latitude, longitude, and altitude. The `trees-fields` function defines the fields used to describe trees throughout the app; other fields get discarded. The `get-trees` function is the subquery used to filter, merge, and refine the estimators about trees.

```
(def geo-tree
  "parses geolocation for tree format"
  (partial re-seq-chunks #"^(\S+),(\S+),(\S+)\s*$"))

(def trees-fields ["?blurb" "?tree_id" "?situs" "?tree_site"
                   "?species" "?wikipedia" "?calflora" "?avg_height"
                   "?tree_lat" "?tree_lng" "?tree_alt" "?geohash"])

(defn get-trees [src tree-meta trap]
  "subquery to parse/filter the tree data"
  (<- trees-fields
    (src ?blurb ?misc ?geo ?kind)
```

```
(re-matches #"^\s+Private.*Tree ID.*" ?misc)
(parse-tree ?misc :> ?priv ?tree_id ?situs
 ?tree_site ?raw_species)
((c/comp s/trim s/lower-case) ?raw_species :> ?species)
(tree-meta ?species ?wikipedia ?calflora
 ?min_height ?max_height)
(avg ?min_height ?max_height :> ?avg_height)
(geo-tree ?geo :> ?tree_lat ?tree_lng ?tree_alt)
((c/each read-string) ?tree_lat ?tree_lng :> ?lat ?lng)
(geo/encode ?lat ?lng geo-precision :> ?geohash)
(:trap (hfs-textline trap))))
```

Note the call (re-matches #"^\s+Private.*Tree ID.*" ?misc) early in the subquery. This regular expression filters records about trees out of the GIS tuple stream. This creates a branch in the Cascading flow diagram.

After calling parse-tree to get the tree properties from the raw data, next we use ((c/comp s/trim s/lower-case) ?raw_species :> ?species) to normalize the species name. In other words, force it to lowercase and strip any trailing spaces, so that it can be used in a join. The call to tree-meta performs that join. Next, the call to avg estimates the height for each tree. This is a rough approximation, but good enough to produce a reasonable "shade" metric.

The last few lines clean up the geolocation coordinates. First these coordinates are parsed, then converted from strings to decimal numbers. Then the geo/encode uses the coordinates to create a "geohash" index. A geohash is a string that gives an approximate location. In this case, the six-digit geohash 9q9jh0 identifies a five-block square in which tree 412 is located. That's a good enough approximation to join with other data about that location, later in the workflow.

Finally, the fields defined in trees-fields for tree 412 get structured this way:

```
?blurb      Tree: 412 site 1 at 115 HAWTHORNE AV, on HAWTHORNE AV 22 from pl
?tree_id    412
?situs      115
?tree_site  1
?species    liquidambar styraciflua
?wikipedia  http://en.wikipedia.org/wiki/Liquidambar_styraciflua
?calflora   http://calflora.org/cgi-bin/species_query.cgi?where-calrecnum=8598
?avg_height 27.5
?tree_lat   37.446001565119
?tree_lng   -122.167713417554
?tree_alt   0.0
?geohash    9q9jh0
```

At this point we have a data product for trees. Figure 8-2 shows a conceptual flow diagram for the part of the workflow that structured this data.

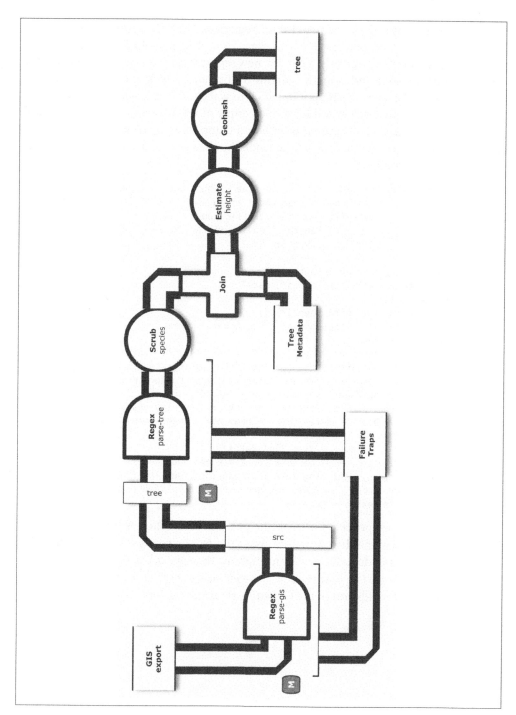

Figure 8-2. Conceptual flow diagram for tree data

Next we repeat many of the same steps for the road data. The GIS export is more complex for roads than for trees because the roads are described per block, with each block divided into segments. Effectively, there is a new segment recorded for every turn in the road. Road data also includes metrics about traffic rates, pavement age and type, etc. Our goal is to find a quiet shady spot in which to walk and take a cell phone call. So we can leverage the road data per segment in a couple of ways. Let's create one estimator to describe how quiet each segment is based on comparing the traffic types and rates. Then we'll create another estimator to describe the shade based on comparing how the pavement reflects sunlight.

```
(def roads-fields ["?road_name" "?bike_lane" "?bus_route" "?truck_route"
                   "?albedo" "?road_lat" "?road_lng" "?road_alt" "?geohash"
                   "?traffic_count" "?traffic_index" "?traffic_class"
                   "?paving_length" "?paving_width" "?paving_area"
                   "?surface_type"])

(defn get-roads [src road-meta trap]
  "subquery to parse/filter the road data"
  (<- roads-fields
      (src ?road_name ?misc ?geo ?kind)
      (re-matches #"^\s+Sequence.*Traffic Count.*" ?misc)
      (parse-road ?misc :>
                  ?traffic_count ?traffic_index ?traffic_class
                  ?paving_length ?paving_width ?paving_area ?surface_type
                  ?overlay_year_str ?bike_lane ?bus_route ?truck_route)
      (road-meta ?surface_type ?albedo_new ?albedo_worn)
      ((c/each read-string) ?overlay_year_str :> ?overlay_year)
      (estimate-albedo ?overlay_year ?albedo_new ?albedo_worn :> ?albedo)
      (bigram ?geo :> ?pt0 ?pt1)
      (midpoint ?pt0 ?pt1 :> ?lat ?lng ?alt)
      ;; why filter for min? because there are geo duplicates..
      ((c/each c/min) ?lat ?lng ?alt :> ?road_lat ?road_lng ?road_alt)
      (geo/encode ?road_lat ?road_lng geo-precision :> ?geohash)
      (:trap (hfs-textline trap))))
```

Similar to the business process for trees, the get-roads function is the subquery used to filter, merge, and refine the estimators about roads. The roads-fields function defines the fields used to describe roads throughout the app; other fields get discarded. The regular expression (re-matches #"^\s+Sequence.*Traffic Count.*" ?misc) filters records about roads out of the GIS tuple stream, creating a branch.

We use some metadata about roads, in this case just to infer metrics about the pavement reflecting sunlight. As pavement ages, its albedo properties change. So we parse the `surface_type` and `overlay_year`, then call `road-meta` to join with metadata. Then we can estimate albedo to describe how much a road segment reflects sunlight.

Note that there are some duplicates in the geo coordinates for road segments. We use (`c/each c/min`) to take the minimum value for each segment, reducing the segment list to unique values. Then we use `geo/encode` to create a six-digit geohash for each segment.

Great—now we have another data product, for roads. Figure 8-3 shows a conceptual flow diagram for the part of the workflow that structured and enriched this data.

The following tuple shows the road segment located nearest to tree 412—note that the geohash matches, because they are within the same bounding box:

```
?blurb         Hawthorne Avenue from Alma Street to High Street
?traffic_count 3110
?traffic_class local residential
?surface_type  asphalt concrete
?albedo        0.12
?min_lat       37.446140860599854
?min_lng       -122.1674652295435
?min_alt       0.0
?geohash       9q9jh0
```

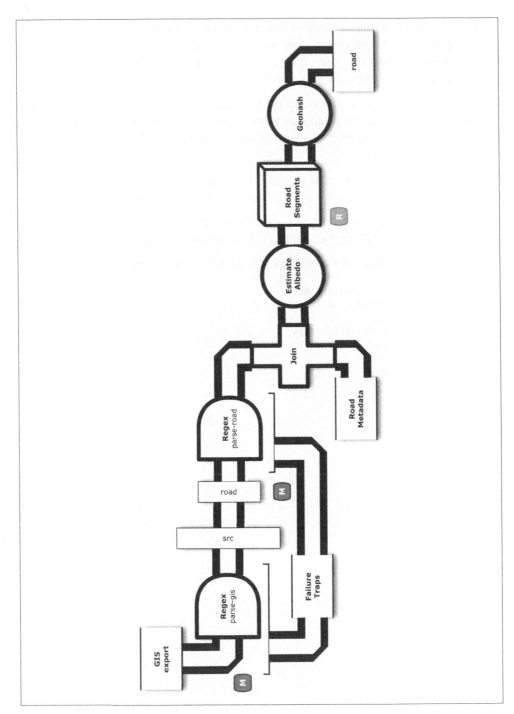

Figure 8-3. Conceptual flow diagram for road data

Calibrating Metrics for the Recommender

A good next step is to use an analytics tool such as R to analyze and visualize the data about trees and roads. We do that step to perform calibration and testing of the data products so far. Take a look at the *src/scripts/copa.R* file, which is an R script to analyze tree and road data.

For example, Figure 8-4 shows a chart for the distribution of tree species in Palo Alto. American sweetgum (*Liquidambar styraciflua*) is the most common tree.

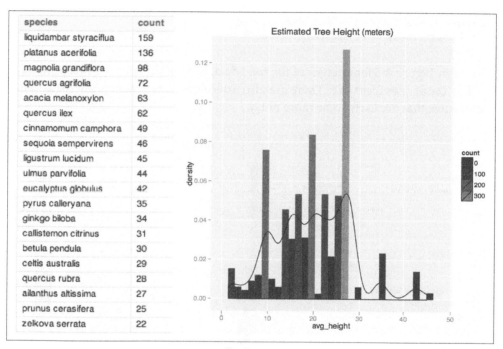

species	count
liquidambar styraciflua	159
platanus acerifolia	136
magnolia grandiflora	98
quercus agrifolia	72
acacia melanoxylon	63
quercus ilex	62
cinnamomum camphora	49
sequoia sempervirens	46
ligustrum lucidum	45
ulmus parvifolia	44
eucalyptus globulus	42
pyrus calleryana	35
ginkgo biloba	34
callistemon citrinus	31
betula pendula	30
celtis australis	29
quercus rubra	28
ailanthus altissima	27
prunus cerasifera	25
zelkova serrata	22

Figure 8-4. Summary analysis for tree data

Also, there's a density plot/bar chart of estimated tree heights, most of which are in the 10- to 30-meter range. Palo Alto is known for many tall eucalyptus and sequoia trees (the city name translates to "Tall Stick"), and these show up on the right side of the density plot—great for lots of shade. Overall, the distribution of trees shows a wide range of estimated heights, which helps confirm that our approximation is reasonable to use.

```
library(ggplot2)

dat_folder <- "~/src/concur/CoPA/out"
d <- read.table(file=paste(dat_folder, "tree/part-00000", sep="/"),
              sep="\t", quote="", na.strings="NULL", header=FALSE,
              encoding="UTF8")
```

```
colnames(d) <- c("blurb", "tree_id", "situs", "tree_site", "species",
                 "wikipedia", "calflora", "avg_height", "tree_lat",
                 "tree_lng", "tree_alt", "geohash")

# plot density for estimated tree heights
m <- ggplot(d, aes(x=avg_height))
m <- m + ggtitle("Estimated Tree Height (meters)")
m + geom_histogram(aes(y = ..density.., fill = ..count..)) + geom_density()

# which are the most popular trees?
t <- sort(table(d$species), decreasing=TRUE)
trees <- head(as.data.frame.table(t), n=20)
colnames(trees) <- c("species", "count")
trees
```

Looking at Figure 8-5 for analysis of the road data, most of the road segments are classified as local residential. There are also arteries and collectors (busy roads) plus truck routes that are likely to be more noisy.

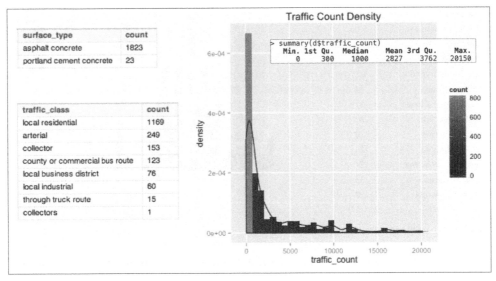

Figure 8-5. Summary analysis for road data

We also see a distribution with a relatively long tail for traffic counts. Using traffic classes and traffic counts as estimators seems reasonable.

```
d <- read.table(file=paste(dat_folder, "road/part-00000", sep="/"),
                sep="\t", quote="", na.strings="NULL", header=FALSE,
                encoding="UTF8")

colnames(d) <- c("road_name", "bike_lane", "bus_route", "truck_route",
                 "albedo", "road_lat", "road_lng", "road_alt", "geohash",
```

```
                      "traffic_count", "traffic_index", "traffic_class",
                      "paving_length", "paving_width", "paving_area",
                      "surface_type")

t <- sort(table(d$surface_type), decreasing=TRUE)
roads <- head(as.data.frame.table(t), n=20)
colnames(roads) <- c("surface_type", "count")
roads

summary(d$traffic_class)
t <- sort(table(d$traffic_class), decreasing=TRUE)
roads <- head(as.data.frame.table(t), n=20)
colnames(roads) <- c("traffic_class", "count")
roads

summary(d$traffic_count)
plot(ecdf(d$traffic_count))

m <- ggplot(d, aes(x=traffic_count))
m <- m + ggtitle("Traffic Count Density")
m + geom_histogram(aes(y = ..density.., fill = ..count..)) + geom_density()
```

Spatial Indexing

Because we are working with GIS data, the attributes that tie together tree data, road data, and GPS track are obviously the geo coordinates: latitude, longitude, and altitude. Much of Palo Alto is relatively flat and not far above sea level because it is close to San Francisco Bay. To make this code a bit simpler, we can ignore altitude. However, we'll need to do large-scale joins and queries based on latitude and longitude. Those are problematic at scale: they are represented as decimal values, and range queries will be required, both of which make parallelization difficult at scale. So we've used a geohash as an approximate location, as a kind of bounding box: it combines the decimal values for latitude and longitude into a string. That makes joins and queries much simpler and makes the app more reasonable to parallelize. Effectively we cut the entire map of Palo Alto into bounding boxes and then compute for each bounding box in parallel.

There can be problems with this approach. For instance, what if the center of a road segment is right in between two geohash squares? We might end up with joins that reference only half the trees near that road segment. There are a number of more interesting algorithms to use for spatial indexing. R-trees (*http://en.wikipedia.org/wiki/R-tree*) is one common approach. The general idea would be to join a given road segment with trees in its bounding box plus the neighboring bounding boxes. Then we apply a better algorithm within those collections of data. The problem is still reasonably constrained and can be parallelized.

In this sample app, we simply consider each geohash value as a kind of "bucket." Imagine that all the data points that fall into the same bucket get evaluated together. Figure 8-6 shows how each block of a road is divided into road segments.

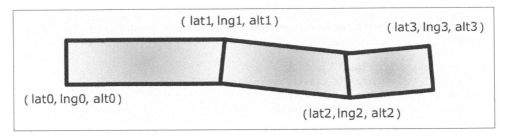

Figure 8-6. Road segments

Our app analyzes each road segment as a data tuple, calculating a center point for each. We use a geohash value to construct a bounding box around that center point, then join the data to collect metrics for all the trees nearby, as Figure 8-7 shows.

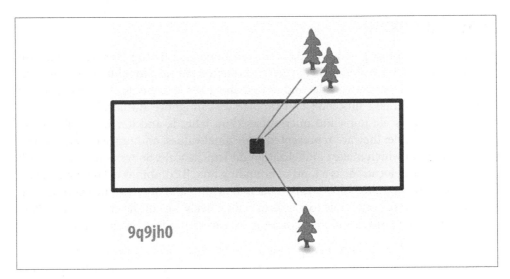

Figure 8-7. Trees near road segments

The join occurs in the `get-shade` function where both the roads and trees tuples reference the `?geohash` field:

```
(defn tree-distance [tree_lat tree_lng road_lat road_lng]
  "calculates distance from a tree to the midpoint of a road segment"
  (let [y (- tree_lat road_lat)
        x (- tree_lng road_lng)]
    (Math/sqrt (+ (Math/pow y 2.0) (Math/pow x 2.0)))))
```

```
(defn get-shade [trees roads]
  "subquery to join the tree and road estimates, to maximize for shade"
  (<- [?road_name ?geohash ?road_lat ?road_lng ?road_alt
       ?road_metric ?tree_metric]
    ((select-fields roads ["?road_name" "?albedo" "?road_lat" "?road_lng"
      "?road_alt" "?geohash" "?traffic_count" "?traffic_class"])
     ?road_name ?albedo ?road_lat ?road_lng ?road_alt ?geohash
     ?traffic_count ?traffic_class)
    (road-metric ?traffic_class ?traffic_count ?albedo :> ?road_metric)
    ((select-fields trees ["?avg_height" "?tree_lat" "?tree_lng"
                           "?tree_alt" "?geohash"])
     ?height ?tree_lat ?tree_lng ?tree_alt ?geohash)
    (> ?height 2.0) ;; limit to trees which are higher than people
    (tree-distance ?tree_lat ?tree_lng ?road_lat ?road_lng :> ?distance)
    (<= ?distance 25.0) ;; one block radius (not in meters)
    (/ ?height ?distance :> ?tree_moment)
    (c/sum ?tree_moment :> ?sum_tree_moment)
    (/ ?sum_tree_moment 200000.0 :> ?tree_metric)))
```

This approach is inclusive, so we get more data than we need. Let's filter out the trees that won't contribute much shade. The call to (> ?height 2.0) limits the trees to those that are taller than people, i.e., those that provide shade. The tree-distance function calculates a distance-to-midpoint from each tree to the road segment's center point. Note that this is not in meters. The call to (<= ?distance 25.0) limits the trees to those within a one-block radius. The distance-to-midpoint calculation is used to filter trees that are too small or too far away to provide shade.

The next step is a trick borrowed from physics. We calculate a sum of moments based on tree height and distance-to-midpoint, then use that as an estimator for shade. The dimensions of this calculation are not particularly important, so long as we get a distribution of estimator values to use for ranking. The R script in *src/scripts/metrics.R* shows some analysis and visualization of this sum of moments. Based on the median of its distribution, we use 200000.0 to scale the estimator—to make its values simpler to understand and compare with other metrics.

The road-metric function calculates metrics for comparing road segments. We have three properties known about each road segment that can be used to create estimators:

```
(defn road-metric [traffic_class traffic_count albedo]
  "calculates a metric for comparing road segments"
  [[(condp = traffic_class
      "local residential"      1.0
      "local business district" 0.5
      0.0)
    (-> traffic_count (/ 200.0) (Math/log) (/ 5.0))
    (- 1.0 albedo)]])
```

First, the traffic class has two values, local residential and local business dis trict, which represent reasonably quiet places to walk—while the other possible values are relatively busy and noisy. So we map from the traffic_class labels to numeric values. Second, the traffic counts get scaled, based on their distribution—similarly to make their values simpler to understand and compare with other metrics. Third, the albedo value needs a sign change but otherwise works directly as an estimator.

In practice, we might train a predictive model—such as a decision tree—to compare these estimators. That could help incorporate customer feedback, QA for the data, etc. Having three estimators to compare road segments—to rank the final results—works well enough for this example. The following tuple shows the resulting metrics for the road segment located nearest to tree 412:

```
?road_name    Hawthorne Avenue from Alma Street to High Street
?geohash      9q9jh0
?road_lat     37.446140860599854
?road_lng     -122.1674652295435
?road_alt     0.0
?road_metric  [1.0 0.5488121277250486 0.88]
?tree_metric  4.36321007861036
```

Figure 8-8 shows the conceptual flow diagram for merging the tree and road metrics to calculate estimators for each road segment.

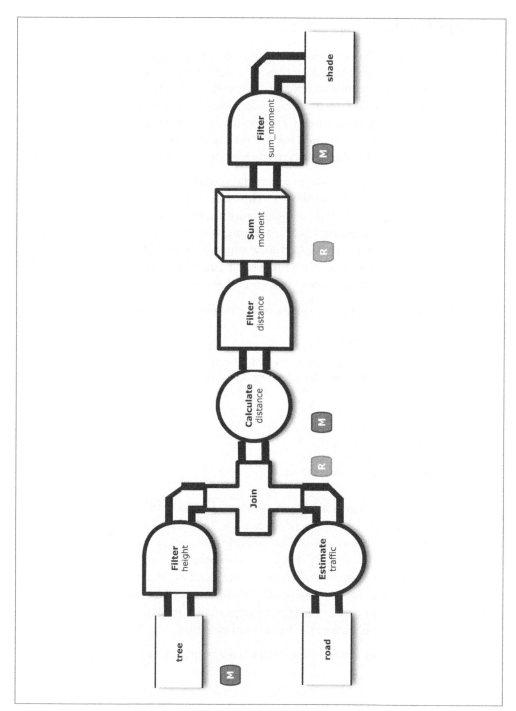

Figure 8-8. Conceptual flow diagram for shade metrics

Personalization

The steps in our app so far have structured the Open Data (GIS export), merged it with curated metadata, then calculated metrics to use for ranking recommendations. That unit of work created data products about quiet shady spots in Palo Alto in which to walk and take a cell phone call. Given different data sources, the same approach could be used for GIS export from other cities. Of course the distribution of geohash values would change, but the business logic would remain the same. In other words, the same work-flow could scale to include many different cities in parallel—potentially, even worldwide.

Our next step is to incorporate the machine data component, namely the log files collected from GPS tracks on smartphones. This data serves to personalize the app, selecting recommendations for the road segments nearest to where the app's users tend to walk. For this example, we had people walking around Palo Alto with their iPhones recording GPS tracks. Then those files were downloaded and formatted as logs. The *data/gps.csv* file shows a sample. Each tuple has a timestamp (`date`), a unique identifier for the user (`uuid`), geo coordinates, plus measurements for movement at that point.

The function `get-gps` is a Cascalog subquery that parses those logs:

```
(defn get-gps [gps_logs trap]
  "subquery to aggregate and rank GPS tracks per user"
  (<- [?uuid ?geohash ?gps_count ?recent_visit]
      (gps_logs ?date ?uuid ?gps_lat ?gps_lng ?alt
        ?speed ?heading ?elapsed ?distance)
      (read-string ?gps_lat :> ?lat)
      (read-string ?gps_lng :> ?lng)
      (geohash ?lat ?lng :> ?geohash)
      (c/count :> ?gps_count)
      (date-num ?date :> ?visit)
      (c/max ?visit :> ?recent_visit)
  ))
```

The function calculates a geohash, then aggregates some of the other values to create estimators. For instance, the call to (`c/count :> ?gps_count`) counts the number of visits, per user, to the same location. That provides an estimator for the "popularity" of each location. The call to (`c/max ?visit :> ?recent_visit`) aggregates the timestamps, finding the most recent visit per user, per location. That provides an estimator for the "recency" of each location. Given the identifiers `uuid` and `geohash`, plus the two metrics `gps_count` and `recent_visit`, we can join the GPS data with the data product for road segments to apply a form of behavioral targeting.

Figure 8-9 shows the conceptual flow diagram for preparing the GPS tracks data.

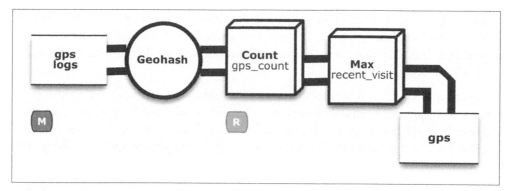

Figure 8-9. Conceptual flow diagram for GPS tracks

The following data shows some of the results near our geohash 9q9jh0 example. Note how the 9q9 prefix identifies neighboring geohash values:

?uuid	?geohash	?gps_count	?recent_visit
342ac6fd3f5f44c6b97724d618d587cf	9q9htz	4	1972376690969
32cc09e69bc042f1ad22fc16ee275e21	9q9hv3	3	1972376670935
342ac6fd3f5f44c6b97724d618d587cf	9q9hv3	3	1972376691356
342ac6fd3f5f44c6b97724d618d587cf	9q9hv6	1	1972376691180
342ac6fd3f5f44c6b97724d618d587cf	9q9hv8	18	1972376691028
342ac6fd3f5f44c6b97724d618d587cf	9q9hv9	7	1972376691101
342ac6fd3f5f44c6b97724d618d587cf	9q9hvb	22	1972376691010
342ac6fd3f5f44c6b97724d618d587cf	9q9hwn	13	1972376690782
342ac6fd3f5f44c6b97724d618d587cf	9q9hwp	58	1972376690965
482dc171ef0342b79134d77de0f31c4f	9q9jh0	15	1972376952532
b1b4d653f5d9468a8dd18a77edcc5143	9q9jh0	18	1972376945348

Great, now we have a data product about areas in Palo Alto that are known to be walkable. Over time, a production app might use this evidence to optimize the workflow.

Recommendations

The last part of this app is the actual recommender. As mentioned earlier, most of the code in the workflow is used for data preparation—recall the 80/20 rule about that. When it comes to the actual recommender, that's just a few lines of code:

```
(defn get-reco [tracks shades]
  "subquery to recommend road segments based on GPS tracks"
  (<- [?uuid ?road ?geohash ?lat ?lng ?alt ?gps_count
       ?recent_visit ?road_metric ?tree_metric]
      (tracks :>> gps-fields)
      (shades ?road ?geohash ?lat ?lng ?alt ?road_metric ?tree_metric)))
```

Mostly this involves a join on geohash fields, then collecting road segment metrics for each user—based on the uuid field. Due to the sparseness of geo coordinates in practice, that join is likely to be efficient. For example, if the mobile app using this data gains millions of users, then the road segment data could be placed in the righthand side (RHS) of the join. Each geohash is a five-block radius, which implies hundreds of road segments or less. That allows for a `HashJoin` as a replicated join that runs more efficiently in parallel at scale.

At this point, we have recommendations to feed into a data API for a mobile app. In other words, per `uuid` value we have a set of recommended road segments. Each road segment has metrics for aggregate tree shade, road reflection, traffic class, traffic rate—in addition to the personalization metrics of recency and popularity for walking near that location.

Recommenders generally combine multiple signals, such as the six metrics we have for each road segment. Then they rank the metrics to personalize results. Some people might prefer recency of visit, others might prefer as little traffic as possible. By providing a tuple of those metrics to the end use case, the mobile app could allow people to adjust their own preferences. In the case of our earlier example, the recommender results nearest to tree 412 are as shown in Table 8-1.

Table 8-1. Example results from recommender

Label	Value
tree	413 site 2
addr	115 Hawthorne Ave
species	Liquidambar styraciflua
geohash	9q9jh0
lat/lng	37.446, -122.168
est. height	23
shade metric	4.363
traffic	local residential, light traffic
visit recency	1972376952532

That spot happens to be a short walk away from my train stop. Two huge American sweetgum trees provide ample amounts of shade on a quiet block of Hawthorne Avenue, which is a great place to walk and take a phone call on a hot summer day in Palo Alto. (It's also not far from a really great fro-yo shop.)

Build and Run

The build script in *project.clj* looks much like the build in Chapter 5:

```
(defproject cascading-copa "0.1.0-SNAPSHOT"
  :description "City of Palo Alto Open Data recommender in Cascalog"
  :url "https://github.com/Cascading/CoPA"
  :license {:name "Apache License, Version 2.0"
            :url "http://www.apache.org/licenses/LICENSE-2.0"
```

```
                :distribution :repo}
      :uberjar-name "copa.jar"
      :aot [copa.core]
      :main copa.core
      :min-lein-version "2.0.0"
      :source-paths ["src/main/clj"]
      :dependencies [[org.clojure/clojure "1.4.0"]
                     [cascalog "1.10.1-SNAPSHOT"]
                     [cascalog-more-taps "0.3.1-SNAPSHOT"]
                     [clojure-csv/clojure-csv "2.0.0-alpha2"]
                     [org.clojars.sunng/geohash "1.0.1"]
                     [date-clj "1.0.1"]]
      :exclusions [org.clojure/clojure]
      :profiles {:dev {:dependencies [[midje-cascalog "0.4.0"]]}
                 :provided {:dependencies
                   [[org.apache.hadoop/hadoop-core "0.20.2-dev"]]
                 }})
```

To build this sample app from a command line, run Leiningen:

```
$ lein clean
$ lein uberjar
```

That builds a "fat jar" that includes all the libraries for the Cascalog app. Next, we clear any previous output directory (required by Hadoop), then run the app in standalone mode:

```
$ rm -rf out/
$ hadoop jar ./target/copa.jar \
    data/copa.csv data/meta_tree.tsv data/meta_road.tsv data/gps.csv \
    out/trap out/park out/tree out/road out/shade out/gps out/reco
```

The recommender results will be in partition files in the *out/reco/* directory. A gist on GitHub (*https://gist.github.com/4641263*) shows building and running this app. If your results look similar, you should be good to go.

Alternatively, if you want to run this app on the Amazon AWS cloud, the steps are the same as for "Example 3 in Scalding: Word Count with Customized Operations" on page 54. First you'll need to sign up for the EMR and S3 services, and also have your credentials set up in the local configuration—for example, in your *~/.aws_cred/* directory. Edit the *emr.sh* Bash script to use one of your S3 buckets, and then run that script from your command line.

Key Points of the Recommender Workflow

This workflow illustrates some of the key points of building Enterprise data workflows:

1. Typically a workflow starts with some kind of ETL, loading unstructured data—which we see for the GIS export and GPS log files.

2. Then we have several steps of data preparation—in other words, creating a data product about shady quiet road segments.

3. From that point, we used R to analyze and visualize the intermediate data—essentially testing and calibrating before setting parameters for the recommender.

4. Next, we leveraged algorithms—geospatial indexing approximated by a geohash, behavioral targeting, plus a replicated join—so that the workflow could run efficiently in parallel at scale.

Another important point is to consider what kinds of data sources were used and what value each contributed. This app shows how to combine three major categories of data:

Open Data
> Unstructured data about municipal infrastructure (trees and roads) exported from the city's GIS systems—which provides the value back to the community

Machine Data
> Unstructured data about where people like to walk, e.g., log files of GPS tracks downloaded from smartphones—which provides the Big Data aspect and drives personalization, giving value to individuals

Curated Metadata
> Structured data (tabular) that allows us to leverage other sources, e.g., make inferences about tree species and road conditions

Open Data practices are relatively recent and evolving rapidly. Ultimately these will include the process of curation, incorporating metadata and ontologies, to help make community uses simpler and more immediate.

Of course, there are plenty of criticisms about this app and ways in which it might be improved. We made assumptions about badly formatted data, simply throwing it away. Some of the tree species names have spelling errors or misclassifications that could be cleaned up and provided back to the City of Palo Alto to improve its GIS. Certainly there are more sophisticated ways to handle the geospatial work. Arguably, this app was intended as a base to build upon for student projects. The workflow can be extended to include more data sources and produce different kinds of recommendations.

As an example of extending the app, the data products could be even more valuable if there were estimators for ambient noise levels based on time and location. So how could we get that? This app infers noise from data about road segments: traffic classes, traffic rates. We could take it a step further and adjust the traffic rates using statistical models based on time of day, and perhaps infer from bus lines, train schedules, etc. We might be able to pull in data from other APIs, such as Google Maps. Thinking a bit more broadly, we might be able to purchase aggregate data from other sources, such as business security networks, where cameras have audio feeds. Or perhaps we could sample audio levels from mobile devices, in exchange for some kind of credits. Large telecoms use techniques like that to build their location services.

Some of the extensions that have been suggested so far include the following:

City of Palo Alto
Help assess the impact of new zoning and building permits; e.g., are there poisonous trees near a proposed day care center?

Calflora
Report concentrations of invasive trees or endangered species, or perhaps optimize where to release beneficial insects.

Real estate
Optimize sales leads by comparing estimated allergy zones with buyers' preferences.

Start-ups
Some invasive tree species have valuable by-products like medicine, whereas others can be converted to biodiesel for targeted harvest services.

Quite a large number of data APIs are available that could be leveraged to extend this app:

- Factual (*http://developer.factual.com/*) for place data—along with CityGrid, Foursquare, Yelp, Localeze, YP, etc.
- Trulia (*http://developer.trulia.com/page/gallery*) for neighborhood data, housing prices, etc.
- Google (*https://developers.google.com/maps/*) for maps, photos, geocoding, etc.
- Wunderground (*http://www.wunderground.com/weather/api/*) for local weather data
- WalkScore (*http://bit.ly/14O1Ogo*) for neighborhood data and walkability metrics
- GeoWordNet (*http://geowordnet.semanticmatching.org/*) for semantic knowledge base about localized terms
- Various photo sharing APIs and Facebook Graph API in general
- Beer (*http://beermapping.com/api/*)…need we say more?

The leverage for Open Data is about evolving feedback loops. This area represents a greenfield for new approaches, new data sources, and new use cases. Overall, the app shown here provides an interesting example to use for think-out-of-the-box exercises. Fork it on GitHub and show us a new twist.

Troubleshooting Workflows

The following tips are intended to help troubleshoot common issues when people are first working with Cascading. These points are mostly about running the examples in the book, but they apply to Enterprise use cases in general.

Build and Runtime Problems

One of the most frequent and useful tips given to people who are new to Cascading—and to Apache Hadoop in general—is that if your build isn't working as expected, you may need to delete the local Maven repo.

On a Linux or Mac OS X laptop, that purge is handled by:

```
$ rm -rf ~/.m2
```

The build systems mentioned in this book—Gradle, Leiningen, SBT—all depend on Maven under the hood. Unfortunately, sometimes Maven gets stuck. Purge its local repository, and then run your build again.

Another common issue with builds is that the Hadoop distribution—or other included JARs—has a dependency conflict with the Cascading artifacts in the Maven repo that you're using. For example, most of the builds shown in this book require `cascading-core` and `cascading-hadoop` for compile-time dependencies. The builds that include unit tests will also depend on `cascading-test`, `junit`, etc. Depending on your deployment environment, some artifacts may need to be excluded, e.g., logging.

Other typical problems encountered include the following:

- Using Java 7—should use Java 6 instead
- Using a Hadoop version higher than 1.x—see the Cascading compatibility matrix (*http://cascading.org/support/compatibility/*)

- Installing Hadoop but not in "standalone" mode
- Running Hadoop atop Cygwin on Windows—which generally does not work
- Installing Hadoop using Homebrew on Mac OS X—install from the Apache Hadoop download or one of the other major distributions instead

Anti-Patterns

Some patterns of coding are counterproductive and generally indicate that the design of an app should be reworked. We call these anti-patterns, and some are specific to Cascading.

If you find that you are writing substantial amounts of custom operations to make a Cascading app perform the business process you need, that's a warning sign. We find that most Cascading apps require few custom operations, unless a developer is trying to end-around the pattern language.

Another anti-pattern concerns traps. These are intended for exceptional data—rare, unintended edge cases in the tuple stream. If you find that traps are being used in an app to define the business process, that's a warning sign. Filters and branches are supposed to be used to direct the tuple flows—for those tuples that are not exceptions. Apps will not perform well when traps get used in place of filters.

Factory methods represent another kind of anti-pattern. Instead use SubAssembly subclasses. The object constructors in Cascading are "factories," so there's not much sense in adding unneeded code that in turn makes the app harder to understand. That would be an example of introducing accidental complexity.

Workflow Bottlenecks

Performing aggregations at scale on Apache Hadoop is a hard problem. Joins in particular can be difficult, and Cascading provides alternatives to improve performance. In Chapter 3 we used HashJoin for a replicated join—in the case where one side is smaller than the other. Otherwise, the join must be based on a CoGroup and the developer may need to adjust the threshold for spilling to disk.

There also are many third-party extensions to Cascading, some of which can improve the performance of large joins. For example, BloomJoin is a drop-in replacement for CoGroup, based on using a bloom filter built from the righthand side (RHS) keys. This can improve performance significantly when the RHS is relatively small but the RHS tuples won't fit in memory (*http://bit.ly/165JxKD*).

Another typical performance problem with Hadoop jobs concerns aggregations in general--key/value skew. Consider the social graph for a social network such as Twitter:

most people may have up to a few hundred followers, but then a few outliers such as Lady Gaga may have millions. This can cause a highly skewed distribution of values per key during the reduce tasks. The effect is that many tasks will start during a reduce phase, and most finish relatively quickly. A few "straggler" tasks—e.g., Lady Gaga's set of followers—continue processing, perhaps for many hours. Overall the cluster utilization metrics drop because only a few tasks are running; however, the app itself cannot progress until all of its reduce tasks complete. A potential workaround is to filter the outlier keys that have huge sets of values and process them in a different branch of the app.

Other Resources

This book is intended to be an introduction to Cascading and related open source projects. There are several resources online for learning about Cascading in much more detail:

- User Guide (*http://docs.cascading.org/cascading/2.1/userguide/htmlsingle/*)
- JavaDoc API Guide (*http://docs.cascading.org/cascading/2.1/javadoc/*)
- SDK and Sample Apps (*http://cascading.org/sdk/*)
- Extensions (*http://cascading.org/extensions/*)
- Conjars Maven repo (*http://conjars.org/*)

Also, there are a wealth of Cascading users and active discussions on the `cascading-user` email forum (*http://bit.ly/19U7Lvl*). If you have a problem with a Cascading app —or Cascalog, Scalding, PyCascading, Cascading.JRuby, etc.—then generate your flow diagram as a DOT file and post a note to the email list.

Index

We'd like to hear your suggestions for improving our indexes. Send email to index@oreilly.com.

Sujit Pal, 59
system integration, viii

T

tap identifier, 13, 55
test-driven development, xi, 28, 41, 48, 49, 78
text analytics, 21
TextDelimited, 3, 55, 69
TF-IDF, 33, 74
The Climate Corporation, xii, 79
Think Big Analytics, 59
Thor Olavsrud, x
Thrift, 13
Tim Berglund, 5
Tom White, 1
topology, 4, 79
traps, 44, 50, 74
Tridivesh Jena, 106
TSV, 3, 55, 56, 69
tuple schema, 3, 12, 19, 55, 68
Twitter, xvi, 48, 54, 56, 66, 69, 79
type-safe API, 58

U

UDFs, 22, 28, 30, 58, 79
unit tests, 21, 41, 49, 77
user-defined functions, 22
uSwitch, 69, 79

V

Vijay Srinivas Agneeswaran, xviii
Viswa Sharma, xviii

W

Wen-Ching Lin, 106
William Back, 92
Word Count, 8, 17, 27, 74
workflow, 3, 72, 76

Y

Yahoo!, xv, 29
Yieldbot, 80

About the Author

Paco Nathan is a Data Scientist at Concurrent, Inc., and heads up the developer outreach program there. He has a dual background from Stanford in math/stats and distributed computing, with 25+ years of experience in the tech industry. As an expert in Hadoop, R, predictive analytics, machine learning, and natural language processing, Paco has built and led several expert Data Science teams, with data infrastructure based on large-scale cloud deployments. He has presented twice on the AWS Start-Up Tour, and gives talks often about Hadoop, Data Science, and Cloud Computing.

Colophon

The animal on the cover of *Enterprise Data Workflows with Cascading* is the Atlantic cod (*Gadus morhua*).

The cover image is from an unknown source. The cover font is Adobe ITC Garamond. The text font is Adobe Minion Pro; the heading font is Adobe Myriad Condensed; and the code font is Dalton Maag's Ubuntu Mono.

Have it your way.

Get even more
for your money.

Join the O'Reilly Community, and register the O'Reilly books you own. It's free, and you'll get:

- $4.99 ebook upgrade offer
- 40% upgrade offer on O'Reilly print books
- Membership discounts on books and events
- Free lifetime updates to ebooks and videos
- Multiple ebook formats, DRM FREE
- Participation in the O'Reilly community
- Newsletters
- Account management
- 100% Satisfaction Guarantee

Signing up is easy:

1. **Go to: oreilly.com/go/register**
2. **Create an O'Reilly login.**
3. **Provide your address.**
4. **Register your books.**

Note: English-language books only

To order books online:
oreilly.com/store

For questions about products or an order:
orders@oreilly.com

To sign up to get topic-specific email announcements and/or news about upcoming books, conferences, special offers, and new technologies:
elists@oreilly.com

For technical questions about book content:
booktech@oreilly.com

To submit new book proposals to our editors:
proposals@oreilly.com

O'Reilly books are available in multiple DRM-free ebook formats. For more information:
oreilly.com/ebooks

Spreading the knowledge of innovators   oreilly.com

Lightning Source UK Ltd.
Milton Keynes UK
UKOW06f0604170913

217345UK00015B/28/P